The Silent Change

ESTEBAN MAGNANI

The Silent Change

Recovered Businesses
in Argentina

t E S E O

"I no longer like people who don't get involved, who don't care about others."

– Miguel Rodríguez, father of Teresa Rodríguez, taken from the book "La política está en otra parte" (Politics is Somewhere Else), *by Hernán López Echagüe, 2002*

Magnani, Esteban
    The silent change : recovered businesses in Argentina . - 1a ed. -
Buenos Aires : Teseo, 2009.
    168 p. ; 23x15 cm.

    Traducido por: Steve Herrick
    ISBN 978-987-1354-31-3

    1. Movimientos Sociales. I. Herrick, Steve, trad.
    CDD 304

ISBN 978-987-1354-31-3
Editorial Teseo

Translated by Steve Herrick

Hecho el depósito que previene la ley 11.723

Para sugerencias o comentarios acerca del contenido de esta obra, escríbanos a:
info@editorialteseo.com

www.editorialteseo.com

To Bar, Leri and Gaspar.

TABLE OF CONTENTS

Prologue to the English Version

By Brendan Martin,
founder and president of the Working World/La Base Foundation

In 2001, the economy of Argentina crashed on a scale that seemed unimaginable at the time. The crisis was caused by a financial disaster born of bad loans and a speculation-driven, bubble economy. In 2009, this formula for crisis sounds eerily familiar to people all around the world, and particularly in the United States. The parallels are dead-on: in the interim eight years, sober economists warned repeatedly that the US economy bore grave similarities to the doomed Argentine one. And yet, the policymakers and plutocrats continued to ride the train of speculation until it, and the world economy, also hit a wall.

The mirror that Argentina's experience offers for the rest of us has never been more obvious nor more important. Among all the lessons to be learned by looking in this mirror (mostly of what not to do, and mostly ignored), likely the most historically significant did not come from the leaders and politicians on high, but from the newly unemployed workers themselves. Sitting outside shuttered factories, workers laid idle by a dysfunctional financial system decided to go back in and work, convention be damned. In doing this, they ignored the dictates of accountants and entrepreneurs and the warnings of policemen and politicians, and they singlehandedly overcame the reputedly inexorable force of a downward business cycle that has so confounded our economic system, its theoreticians, and its trillion dollar bailouts. They entered, they produced, they bartered, and they sold, all on their own, while the "normal" economy continued to die around them. This is the story of the recovered factories, or the "Silent Change," as Esteban has named it.

The change was relatively silent, as often apolitical workers humbly struggled simply to return to work, and the loudest sounds were usually those of the machines they turned back on. But the impact of their actions is immeasurable, and it may prove the only force as powerfully creative as the bursting of the bubble was destructive. With almost no resources, these workers shattered the logic of the system on which their economy was built. Conventional economic wisdom said these worker-run companies shouldn't exist – business must shrink in a downturn, workers must be managed by capital, jobs must be created by entrepreneurs, government must privilege. And yet here they were, often groups of the lowest-level employees, unable to find new work, surrounded by a morbidly broken economy, producing and thriving. Eight years later, their numbers have only grown, their businesses have only become more solid, and the microeconomic engines they restarted have shown no signs of stopping, not even in this new crisis (see the newly written chapter at the end of the book for an update on the situation).

As this introduction is being written, the rich countries of the world are claiming to search their souls to find new ways to avoid catastrophe. And yet, thus far, nothing new has been offered: the continued wisdom is that the banks, the investors, and the wealthy must be saved in order to save the rest of us, even as more workers continue to enter unemployment lines. The recovered factories have shown this doesn't have to be so. If we want to think outside the box of how to "prime the pump" of the economy or how to create a works program, the workers of Argentina have shown us the possibility of a powerful new alternative. If our economic dogmas are proven inaccurate by the unlikely actions of these workers, those dogmas must go. We should all have the burning feeling that our options are greater than what we are told.

The workers of Argentina have yet to be trotted out in Davos[1] to inspire new ideas amongst the world's powerful, and it's unlikely that anyone in a position of authority will consider breaking from orthodoxy and encouraging something as radical as worker control and an economy that rises from the bottom. But whether it is in seven months or seventy years, the story of the Argentine workers will stand as part of history, ready to speak to us when we are ready to listen.

Many people, including me, have worked or studied extensively with the recovered factories. Out of all of us, there are few with more reason to write their history than Esteban Magnani. He was there in the beginning, when, in 2002, he helped create the documentary "The Take" with a team of people researching the factories over the course of years. He followed this up with his own research project, the first edition of this book. For the subsequent five years, he has been working with me and others at the Working World, a non-profit that gives fair credit to worker-run companies and helps them grow and prosper in an often hostile world (see the new chapter at the end for more details on Esteban's current work). His seven years of experience in this movement have given him both an overhead

---

[1]   Editor's note: Davos is a municipality in Switzerland, famous for hosting the annual World Economic Forum, where elite politicians and businesspeople meet.

view and unmatched hands-on experience, and his background in journalism provides learned research and incisive prose. As my colleague and good friend, I want to thank him for writing this book, and helping to share this living history with a world hungry for ideas.

February 2009

Argentina

TRANSLATOR'S FORWARD

By Steve Herrick

From 2006 to 2007, I produced a PDF magazine on fair trade, called *Just Things*. I wanted to promote fair trade, but not as an uncritical cheerleader. Life isn't black and white, and to pretend that any economic model is flawless would show a lack of analytical rigor on my part. The major flaw I saw in fair trade is that it sells itself short by focusing on the "dessert economy" – luxury goods for middle-class consumers in the North, like coffee, ethnic clothing, jewelry, artwork, and occasionally bananas or sugar. These are all good things, and I enthusiastically encourage my friends and family to buy them, but there's a limit to how much sugar and jewelry you can buy. If the model doesn't reach beyond the base of consumers with the time, commitment, and disposable income to actively seek out fair-trade goods for their own sake, then it's not much more than a hobby. (Brendan Martin had come to a similar conclusion when he decided to found the Working World.)

In an attempt to define what "fair trade" is, I set out four requirements. First, it was trade that empowered workers. The more directly workers make the decisions that affect them, the better. Second, it empowered consumers to make fully informed decisions, which mostly amounts to a high level of transparency in business practices and marketing. Third, it had to make a good-faith effort not to damage the environment. Fourth, it had to show a preference towards local production for local consumption. This is not a hard-and-fast requirement (coffee, for example, is mostly grown for export), but where there were choices to be made, I preferred to see businesses taking the local option.

Over time, I began to see that the fair-trade movement wasn't the only model that met these requirements, or even necessarily the one that met them most effectively. After much research, I concluded that worker cooperatives represented the model currently doing the best job. To be sure, the fair-trade organizations I knew showed a strong preference for working with worker cooperatives in the global South, but, with the exception of

Equal Exchange, they weren't practicing or promoting worker cooperativism in the North. Since that time, my interest has been refocused on cooperatives, which I consider fair trade, with or without the label. That's how I became interested in translating this book.

I'm grateful to the co-ops I've been able to learn from directly: the Nueva Vida Women's Sewing Co-op in Ciudad Sandino, Nicaragua; the recovered businesses in Buenos Aires, which I had the pleasure of visiting in late 2006; Just Coffee, here in Madison, Wisconsin; and the interpreters' cooperative I'm helping to organize. I also want to congratulate and thank Esteban Magnani for writing this book. I've tried to make sure it's his voice that comes through, not mine. When the nature of translating forced me to make a judgment call, I opted to use everyday language, which I think better reflects the nature of the work and the workers than stiff, academic language.

In solidarity.

February 2009

Presentation and Acknowledgments for the English Version

What you are about to read is the English version of a book originally published in Spanish in Argentina at the end of 2003. The book has been left unchanged except for the case studies, which were too specific to still be relevant and were therefore replaced by an update specially prepared for this version.

Many people have been key to the publication of this book, but I would like to start by mentioning the main characters, the workers themselves, who inspire books and hopes often without even noticing it. Also, to all the people that spent their valuable time conveying to me their experiences and explaining complex ideas.

My deepest thanks also go to Naomi Klein and Avi Lewis, not only for their support in providing me with priceless material for the original version, but also for opening doors for me to a world I had only previously approached in theory. In our country, working on what you like is a dream come true. The idea that I might make a living working for a good cause is something I would never have imagined possible, and it has happened to me twice: when I was a member of "The Take" crew, and since I started working for the Working World/La Base Foundation in December 2004. Its members, Brendan Martin, Julián Massaldi, Lisette Balbachan, Diego Rozengardt, Eleonora Feser and Ethan Earle, have been a great source of ideas and discussions. Ethan is also the person in charge of the final corrections for this book, helping to make my clumsy English a little more reader-friendly.

Also, I need to thank the translators of this book. The first time I could even imagine accessing a wider public by publishing this book in English was when Tatiana Dawn, a reader of my blog (elcambiosilencioso. com.ar), generously offered to translate it. She did a great job, ultimately inspiring Steve Herrick, a professional translator and researcher on recovered factories, to offer to polish some sections and work hard on others to get a version workers from around the world could read. For a long time, we also played with the idea of getting a publisher for the book, but it proved to be harder than expected. Thanks to the efforts of Tatiana and Steve, by the time we finally received some interest from a publishing house the book was already ready.

I also have to thank the many people who read the different versions of the following chapters, providing me with priceless opinions and suggestions, often finding the time by pushing their own occupations aside: my dad, Tete, Guille, Anita, and Eleonora. Also, the lawyer Florencia Kravetz, who found the time to help me navigate to a safe harbor the chapter on the legal issues of recovered factories.

And without the support and patience of my family, especially Bar, this project would have died away sadly.

Keep in mind that what you are about to start reading, up to the chapter entitled "Recovered factories: an update," is the translation of the Spanish version written in 2003.

When Work is a Crime: The Brukman Battle

By Naomi Klein

In 1812, bands of British weavers and knitters raided textile mills and smashed industrial machines with their hammers. According to the Luddites, the new mechanized looms had eliminated thousands of jobs, broken communities, and deserved to be destroyed. The British government disagreed and called in a battalion of 14,000 soldiers to brutally repress the worker revolt and protect the machines.

Fast-forward two centuries to another textile factory, this one in Buenos Aires. At the Brukman factory, which has been producing men's suits for fifty years, it's the riot police who smash the sewing machines and the 58 workers who risk their lives to protect them.

On Monday, the Brukman factory was the site of the worst repression Buenos Aires has seen in almost a year. Police had evicted the workers in the middle of the night and turned the entire block into a military zone guarded by machine guns and attack dogs. Unable to get into the factory and complete an outstanding order for 3,000 pairs of dress trousers, the workers gathered a huge crowd of supporters and announced it was time to go back to work. At 5 pm, 50 middle aged seamstresses in no-nonsense haircuts, sensible shoes and blue work smocks walked up to the black police fence. Someone pushed, the fence fell, and the Brukman women, unarmed and arm in arm, slowly walked through.

They had only taken a few steps when the police began shooting: tear gas, water cannons, first rubber bullets, then lead. The police even charged the Mothers of the Plaza de Mayo, in their white headscarves embroidered with the names of their "disappeared" children. Dozens of demonstrators were injured and police fired tear gas into a hospital where some had taken refuge. This is a snapshot of Argentina less than a week before its presidential elections. Each of the five major candidates is promising to put this crisis-ravaged country back to work. Yet Brukman's workers are treated as if sewing a gray suit were a capital crime.

Why this state Luddism, this rage at machines? Well, Brukman isn't just any factory, it's a *fábrica ocupada*, one of almost 200 factories across the country that have been taken over and run by their workers over the past year and a half. For many, the factories, employing more than 10,000 nationwide and producing everything from tractors to ice cream, are seen not just as an economic alternative, but as a political one as well. "They are afraid of us because we have shown that if we can manage a factory we can also manage a country," Brukman worker Celia Martinez said on Monday night. "That's why this government decided to repress us."

At first glance, Brukman looks like every other garment factory in the world. As in Mexico's hyper-modern maquiladoras and Toronto's crumbling coat factories, Brukman is filled with women hunched over sewing machines, their eyes straining and fingers flying over fabric and thread. What makes Brukman different are the sounds. There is the familiar roar of machines and the hiss of steam, but there is also Bolivian folk music, coming from a small tape deck in the back of the room, and softly spoken voices, as older workers leaned over younger ones, showing them new stitches. "They wouldn't let us do that before," Martinez says. "They wouldn't let us get up from our workspaces or listen to music. But why not listen to music, to lift the spirits a bit?"

Here in Buenos Aires, every week brings news of a new occupation: a four-star hotel now run by its cleaning staff, a supermarket taken by its clerks, a regional airline about to be turned into a cooperative by the pilots and attendants. In small Trotskyist journals around the world, Argentina's occupied factories, where the workers have seized the means of production, are giddily hailed as the dawn of a socialist utopia. In large business magazines like *The Economist*, they are ominously described as a threat to the sacred principle of private property. The truth lies somewhere in between.

In Brukman, for instance, the means of production weren't seized, they were simply picked up after they had been abandoned by their legal owners. The factory had been in decline for several years, debts to utility companies were piling up, and over a period of five months, the seamstresses had seen their salaries slashed from AR$100 a week to a mere two pesos – not enough for bus fare.

On December 18, the workers decided it was time to demand a travel allowance. The owners, pleading poverty, told the workers to wait at the factory while they looked for the money. "We waited for them until evening. We waited until night," Martinez says. "No one came." After getting the keys from the doorman, Martinez and the other workers slept at the factory. They have been running it every since. They have paid the outstanding bills, attracted new clients, and without profits and management salaries to worry about, managed to pay themselves steady salaries. All these decisions have been made democratically, by vote in open assemblies. "I don't know why the owners had such a hard time," Martinez says. "I don't know much about accounting but for me it's easy: addition and subtraction."

Brukman has come to represent a new kind of labor movement here, one that is not based on the power to stop working (the traditional union tactic) but on the dogged determination to keep working no matter what. It's a demand that is not driven by dogmatism but by realism: in a country where 58 per cent of the population is living in poverty, workers know that they are a pay cheque away from having to beg and scavenge to survive. The specter that is haunting Argentina's occupied factories is not communism, but indigence.

But isn't it simple theft? After all, these workers didn't buy the machines, the owners did – if they want to sell them or move them to another country, surely that's their right. As the federal judge wrote in Brukman's eviction order, "Life and physical integrity have no supremacy over economic interests."

Perhaps unintentionally, he has summed up the naked logic of deregulated globalization: capital must be free to seek out the lowest wages and most generous incentives, regardless of the toll that process takes on people and communities.

The workers in Argentina's occupied factories have a different vision. Their lawyers argue that the owners of these factories have already violated basic market principles by failing to pay their employees and their creditors, even while collecting huge subsidies from the State. Why can't the State now insist that the indebted companies' remaining assets continue to serve the public with steady jobs? Dozens of workers' cooperatives have already been awarded legal expropriation. Brukman is still fighting.

Come to think of it, the Luddites made a similar argument in 1812. The new textile mills put profits for a few before an entire way of life. Those textile workers tried to fight that destructive logic by smashing the machines. The Brukman workers have a much better plan: they want to protect the machines and smash the logic.

This article first appeared in The Globe and Mail.

1. Introduction

I think the first time I really understood what it meant to have nothing left to lose was when Cándido, a mild-mannered printer from the Chilavert Cooperative, described to me in his own words his determination to go right to the bitter end. He said, "When I saw the police coming in, I thought, 'if it's not going to be ours, it's not going to be anybody's,' and I prepared a Molotov cocktail to destroy all our equipment." I told Cándido he would have ended up in prison. "So? Being out on the street, unemployed, is the same thing at my age." It's true: for this 59-year-old man, as for so many others, the only alternative to ending up penniless or with a pittance from a work plan was to go out and put his life on the line. When these workers finally got the equipment working again, they discovered that they were no longer the same people. A change had occurred within them, a transformation that took place somewhere beyond the clamor of the struggle, beyond the anxiety of waiting for another negotiation or figuring out how to get a power supply. A silent change has transformed them and their surroundings. It's allowed them to quiet the voice within telling them their only option was to look out for their individual interests. With no need for speeches or theories, they've managed to build the basis for a profound political change, which is being woven by them and between them, day by day, and which ultimately will weave through all of society. Even now, it renews hope for the rest of us.

There's an old saying that "politics abhors a vacuum." Maybe that's why the seeds of something new are taking root in the political and economic rubble left by thirty years of neoliberalism, seeds of something Argentines couldn't imagine only five years ago, when they drifted among consumerist dreams and homogenized desires. When the crash came, some decided to stop wasting their time on idle accusations against anonymous people and start trying to change the atmosphere asphyxiating their minds. They were determined to create, out of nothing, a space that would let them grow and approach what was once unimaginable. On December 19 and 20,

2001, just after the social explosion, people seemed ready to take the reins of the future through assemblies, mobilization, demands, recovered factories, pickets and a thousand other ways for which there are not words yet.

Today, many of these forms of organization have proven to be ephemeral, but thanks to the social explosion, there are some that have survived. It's hard to imagine evolution without diversity. Without the vacuum left by what came before, what's growing and developing today would have been much more unlikely. Power is once again settling in, though it's hard to say just where. One of the things to happen to this devastated and seemingly sterile country is the appearance of a group of people who are not only making change, but living it, and making a living from it. They ask nothing from anyone. In the worker-controlled enterprises, there is a new way of organizing work, the axis on which the whole social order turns.

Paradoxical as it might seem, the people most opposed to the growth of this force are the very ones that caused the conditions that made it necessary. If they hadn't been so insatiable, the workers wouldn't have gambled the only thing remaining to them – their own lives – to fight to the end in a struggle that seemed suicidal. Thanks to this effort, it's now easier to imagine an alternative to going home empty-handed and unemployed. There are even those who dare to dream greater dreams and imagine a better society. The struggle for work and against unemployment, which fills hundreds of charts and graphs in the media, becomes real when you get to know the life experiences behind the numbers. Sometimes, it's hard to find words to convey the anxiety, the doubts, the injustices and the hunger facing the worker who wants to reclaim a job. Sometimes words are not up to the task any more than grandiose intellectual constructs are.

If you haven't been through the kind of exploitation described in this book, it's an intellectual and sensory challenge to step into this other mindset, where each day might end in a battle where you risk falling across a line from which there may be no return. For almost eight months, I lived with one foot in my own profession, which is made up of words, and the other in the factories, in demonstrations, in discussions with *mate*[2] (invariably sweet) being passed around, running away from tear gas, or in suffocating boredom as we waited for a deputy or senator to raise his manicured hand. Only then could I begin to construct a narrative that might provide a deeper understanding of a group of workers confronting a system that oppressed them, confronting an oppression that was fervently or lazily accepted by most of mainstream society. The workers about whom this book

---

[2]   Editor's note: *Mate* is a traditional drink consumed throughout Argentina, Paraguay, Uruguay and parts of Brazil, among other places. The *mate* itself is a sort of gourd, filled with a shredded tea-like leaf called *yerba*. Hot water is then poured into the *mate* and drank through a straw. *Mate* is enormously popular in Argentina, and many people like to drink it with sugar.

is written decided to punch a hole in this system. And as they crawled through the hole they had punched, they widened it for those who would follow. Together, they stretched the space they had created, little by little, giving themselves more room and more pride.

This story is made up of many fragments, and in it I've discovered the courage of people fighting their last battle, spending the last of their energy struggling against a more powerful enemy, and above all, against a generalized sense that utopias have gone out of style. They face a severe shortage of options, and the recovered factories, for all their limitations and failings, are their last hope for something more than bare-bones survival. The factories are also probably one of the last hopes for a society desperate to chart its own destiny, even if it hasn't yet found a way to navigate such a course. It might or might not seem like a big deal, but 15,000 workers managed to stop clinging to work plans and even made some progress, in spite of resistance from business, the judiciary, economic structures, and even prejudice. Thanks to that decision, they've been able to make these factories grow, create new jobs, and distribute profits equitably in a way that no other well-known, contemporary effort has managed. It's hard to imagine turning back now. This movement seeks to put the workers back in abandoned factories where the equipment will otherwise continue to sit idly or else be sold to the lowest bidder for scrap. If the State and society at large gave it more support, thousands of jobs could be created annually.

Some people argue that these factories have owners, that private property still exists in Argentina, but there's also a counterargument that most bankrupt businesses owe money to their workers, to the State for tax evasion, to banks, and to their suppliers. Who should own these idle factories? Those who hold the deed, or the workers who weren't paid their salaries? Or maybe the State, which didn't make the proprietors pay taxes, allowing them to grow even richer. Or perhaps the banks that gave loans to build the factories, or the citizens that paid taxes that vanished into fraudulent bankruptcies. In this nation, devastated by three decades of neoliberalism and an unprecedented economic crisis, the answer should be clear, even to the capital-less capitalists, who don't respect the very rules of the game they try to impose on others.

When you look at it this way, trying to recover jobs seems like a way of keeping the system going, with self-organized workers in place of corrupt capitalists. It may still work out that way, but the more-or-less explicit goal of a good portion of the people who are reopening factories is to create the material conditions for a change in consciousness to bring about a deeper social change. It's hard to say whether or not they'll reach this goal, because the workers are the ones who are taking power, and they're the ones who will (eventually) have to decide to dedicate the same kind of energy that they devoted to the task of reopening factories towards building a new society.

At any rate, the struggle itself is bringing about a silent change in these men and women, who are realizing what they can do and becoming more ambitious. If they've been able to fill their own plates, why not try to fill the neighbors' plates, too? This new manner of organizing work in assemblies and being in charge of their own destinies has made it hard for them look on injustice in the old passive way without a feeling of complicity. Those that watch them achieve the impossible are inspired by their struggle. These workers rarely have friends in the press; nor are they likely to go to the high-society parties that judges attend, or to chic bars to chat with the country's intellectuals. And that is why I wrote this book. That is why I tried to amplify their voice, a voice that journalists rarely record except to fill a column or two of copy. In his last book, López Echagüe speaks bitterly of

> that flock of journalists and communicators with a propensity for intellectual laziness, for chopping up reality and using the bits and pieces for whatever ends best suit their purpose...[3]

There's a whole different reality in San Martín, in Valentín Alsina, in Neuquén (heading towards Centenario) or in the Once neighborhood of Buenos Aires. To reach it, however, you have to get past the prejudices your own co-workers have built up and break down the barriers imposed by a society shaped by selfishness and hardened by dictatorships, which violated our bodies, and by President Menem's rule, which poisoned our spirit. Having crossed these barriers, I feel obliged to try to balance the scale, to open the windows so that more people on the outside may peer in and perhaps meet the gaze of those on the inside. Only once this process has begun in earnest can we hope to begin re-weaving the fabric of a society torn apart by fear, prejudice, and the need to avoid blame. Or perhaps the truth is simpler. It may be that where these very different realities meet, a lot can be learned from those that fight with no fear because they have nothing left to lose. More and more people can learn to imagine alternatives, perhaps even risking to depend on them to live.

I wrote this book for all these reasons. It's an attempt to capture with pen and ink a piece of the living, breathing history of Argentina, a story that can be read in the hands of the workers. But it can only really be understood up close and personal. In my research, I collected fragments of a story that has yet to come into focus. Even its own main characters can't agree on how to read it. Many of these fragments exist only in the

---

[3]   López Echagüe, 2002.

memories of the participants, in notes in diaries (which can differ or even contradict each other), in some pamphlet, in a meeting captured on film, or just floating for a brief moment on the air. We'll look for common threads that can be woven into a general picture, but for whatever reason – the newness of all this, the diversity of circumstances, or the inexperience of the researcher – the larger tendencies continue to hide behind a curtain of exceptions, making it difficult to draw more definitive conclusions. With all that in mind, this book will be a rough draft for future works that will draw on ever broader experiences; it will be almost a mythology, ready to fight the social imagery of politicians, who talk a lot and say little, and of television programs, which measure personal success in cars and clothes.

I hope the result will be a puzzle, an eye-opener that will (with a little luck) plant doubts in the reader's mind. Hopefully, you will go out and do your own research in the only way some things can be understood – by putting your own beliefs and your own body on the line.

1.1. Possible viewpoints

The phenomenon of recovered factories (like any phenomenon, really) can be seen from countless perspectives. From a short-term historical perspective, for example, it can be analyzed as a kind of "miracle," coming after ten years of Menem's presidency,[4] which left the earth scorched of combativeness, creativity, and any sense of solidarity or struggle. Or, it can be seen in the historical context of several decades of *Peronista* resistance, which provided experience to the most combative sectors of society.

Another possible perspective is the internationalist view (which colors a good part of the creation of this book), brought here by visitors speaking a nearly indecipherable Spanish as they file through the recovered factories to the surprise, delight, and sometimes exhaustion of the workers. With one foot still in their home country, these visitors usually come looking for something genuine, fleeing the suffocation of desires imposed by advertising and the fleeting pleasures of wealthier consumer societies. In the general worldwide crisis of legitimacy that capitalism is currently facing, Argentina – once a pioneer in a neoliberal experiment that brushed aside legitimacy and consensus – is now spearheading a much-needed change that could be considered a test case for the rest of the world.

Closely connected to all of this is that great question mark, representative democracy, of which so many foreign journalists have come in

---

4   Editor's note: Menem is well known for his neoliberal policies, including the deregulation and privatization of vast sectors of Argentina's economy. Many blame him, in large part, for the financial crisis that struck Argentina at the turn of the 21st century.

pursuit. It's certainly been called into question in this country, with good reason –especially after the events of December 19 and 20 – and there's a need to demonstrate that another, more horizontal form of democracy is possible. It's interesting to note that, while representative democracy is being questioned in many societies – as a result of repression, corruption, injustice, blatant crimes, and human suffering – direct democracy still needs to demonstrate its utility and effectiveness. It seems like a hundred times I've described to a friend or acquaintance that the cooperatives make their decisions in assemblies, only to hear, "Yeah, but somebody has to be in charge..." or, "Who's really managing the whole thing?" or, "Somebody's going to come along and gobble them up!" Anyone who's been to assemblies knows that, while there are natural leaders, the practice of holding assemblies gives people the ability to say "no," to express dissent, and to promote their opinion through conviction and not coercion. In those situations in which a small group makes the decisions, there's a tendency to gravitate towards the same dynamics that caused the crisis in the first place, and the survival rate goes back to what it was under earlier models. On the other hand, the co-ops that adapt to the complexity of direct democracy seem to show signs of development. As we walk the path of possible viewpoints, the next step is to look at interpersonal relationships. These infinite encounters can only be classified and described at the risk of stripping them of their very essence: their diversity and individuality. Often, a literary take on things captures this in a way that remains elusive to the academic style. In a meeting at a recovered factory, Osvaldo Bayer said, "What unity, what a sense of poetry, what a sense of beauty, what a sense of struggle! Let's follow their example and fight!"[5] This spirit pervades the factories, where it faces cynicism, but never romanticism. Here, being up-front is a right.

What the academic style can do is give us tools to think things that have never before been thought. On occasion, however, academics deconstruct an idea until there is nothing left of it, leaving us perplexed and empty-handed. Today, there are some intellectuals who have said "mea culpa[6]" and stopped going on about how things should be. For the first time in their lives, they're actually listening to the social classes they've always claimed to defend.

As Naomi Klein said in May 2002, sitting across from the Brukman factory from which the workers had been evicted,

> The idea of this round-table, that so-called intellectuals and journalists should offer theories about how the working class should organize and fight, is both of-

---

[5] "Nuestra lucha" No. 129, 4/2002.
[6] Editor's note: A Latin phrase, meaning "my fault".

fensive and dangerous. This idea is responsible for a lot of what's dysfunctional about the Left today. If there's anything to be learned from these surprising Brukman women, it's that the working class already knows how to organize and fight. In Argentina and around the world, original, creative, effective direct action is way ahead of intellectual leftist theory.

There's also a romantic view that sees steps toward utopia in something that's really nothing more than an attempt to keep a job and keep personal, private consumption going. Not all the workers have the class consciousness or romanticism – sometimes mixed with a vulgar traditionalism – which journalists and other analysts insist on reading into this phenomenon. There are workers that experienced the consequences of neoliberalism up close and personal and still voted for Menem. Others refuse to share their meager unemployment benefits with *compañeros* in need, and still others think about sub-contracting as soon as the cooperative gets going. Of course, there are also workers that dream of a socialist Argentina, but they're not necessarily the majority. To the extent that it's possible to detect a common tendency in such diversity, the cases analyzed below show that the struggle is born of the desire to hold on to possessions and the fear of the worst fate of all: unemployment.

This fear is a powerful motivation, and we shouldn't underestimate it. Class consciousness comes later – in the best of cases – along with a deeper transformation, thanks to the daily practices in a worker-controlled factory, as we'll see later.

All these viewpoints will make appearances in this book, and the reader will have plenty of raw material to come up with even more. In spite of this variety, the story is tied together with an idea that can be summed up in a phrase borrowed from Marxism: You have to go from earth to heaven, not heaven to earth.

> That means that we don't begin with what a person says, imagines, or thinks, nor with what is said, imagined or thought about them to find the flesh-and-blood person. We start from the real, active person in their everyday life, and from there, we follow the development of their ideology and the echoes of their life.[7]

To put it painfully briefly, Marx insists that social relations are ultimately determined by material conditions. While the autonomy of social relations is debatable (and the debates could fill a bibliography thousands of pages long), we will accept the idea in this book, and hope to strengthen it with practical examples. Each page of this book hinges on the idea that social discourse and practices (legal, economic, interpersonal, etc.) cannot remain untouched by the changes in the way people survive, which is to say, the changes in the

---

[7]   Marx, Karl, 1968.

way people work. With a change in work – one of the most essential activities in life – there's also a change in the way workers relate to each other, construct their lives, and understand and face the world. Obviously, the "ideological" result of being able to make decisions about one's own work will vary. It's true that work is not the only determining factor in a person's world view, but it's also true that it's one of the essential activities of daily life, and at least for the working class, it provides a structure that sustains all other activities – family life, recreation, culture, etc.

The effect of restructuring work to be more horizontal ranges from a lukewarm feeling of community with other members of a cooperative to a personal conviction that we are all equal and need to fight for a better world. These individual transformations can eventually bring about deeper changes in the social sphere. "Power is not possessed, it is exercised in different places through social relations,"[8] and these social relations are transforming themselves – and power – to eventually distribute it more equitably. In a social climate where it's been accepted that, most of the time, those who hold power use it against the people, we shouldn't underestimate the transformative power of a successful self-managed project.

As this book is being finished, with the number of workers that have recovered their jobs still tiny compared to the number that haven't, we can already see some effects on society. Even in a stingy evaluation of these changes, we can say that when a business goes bankrupt, there are employees who see worker control as a viable alternative to unemployment, and they inform themselves about how to get it done. There are business owners who see that workers don't depend on them for the privilege of working. There's a possibility of changes in the bankruptcy laws to facilitate worker control in the future (the very fact that this is being discussed can be considered a result of the phenomenon). There are workers in these cooperatives who are sharing their fates with their *compañeros* – they've stopped relating through competition and started feeling the power of solidarity. All these changes may seem unimpressive, but the dynamics being set up (factories opening almost daily thanks to the workers) lead us to expect that the temperature will continue to rise as more examples come along.

The daily practice of self-managed work control changes the way people see the world, and may also explain the varied ways that different participants in this phenomenon approach the world. All of them –workers, judges, neighbors, assembly members, police, and strikers – have tools and personal experiences that allow them to see some things, while keeping them from seeing others. In fact, what's at stake in this great struggle for social change is precisely the ability to name things that

---

[8]   Chavez, María, et al., 2002.

currently have no names, tools, or spaces in which to think about them in our society. Private property itself, the basis of all capitalist construction, is in question.

Here's just one example, given to me by Diego Kravetz, lawyer for the National Movement of Recovered Businesses (NMRB): for a while now, the law has been out of touch with reality and doesn't know what to do in many of the situations it faces. The same thing happens in other social spheres – journalism, economy, and morality give answers that are meant to calm their own consciences and fool themselves in the face of evidence that some things are no longer working, which makes it reactionary to keep believing in them.

This book will try to name some of the things that seek to be taken into account. In a best-case scenario, they will let us think about society in ways that are more realistic and fruitful than simply using terminology that has lost its meaning and connection to the world around us.

1.2 The conditions of production

> *"This country...!"*
> *– Avi Lewis, repeatedly, during the first half of 2003, in Argentina.*

Much of the material in this book is the result of an investigation carried out over six months for a documentary directed by Avi Lewis and Naomi Klein, two Canadian journalists and analysts that criticize capitalism and the injustices committed by those that follow its logic. Naomi Klein is the author of "No Logo," one of the most important works on the consequences of neoliberal capitalism, not only at the economic level, but culturally as well. This has earned her the highly inaccurate label "leader of the globalphobes." Avi Lewis, for his part, is well-known in Canada as the host of some 500 political debates over the course of three years for the program "Counterspin."

The couple (they're married) visited Argentina in 2002, and after several months, were struck by the number of new forms of social organization that were emerging. They returned at the end of the year, and for much of 2003 they filmed picket lines, recovered factories, assemblies, and all kinds of organizations and people in an attempt to discover an alternative to savage capitalism.

Near the end of our time working together, I talked to them about my interest in writing a book including some of the material we'd gathered and however much more was necessary. The other choice, I told them, was to let all the interesting material we'd compiled, but that wouldn't fit in a documentary of less than two hours, disappear without a trace. To my delight, they said they didn't consider the information their property and fully supported the idea.

Because Naomi and Avi did many of the interviews that appear in this book, it seemed only fair to name them. In a lot of cases, I was actually their interpreter, and we often talked about our impressions. Most of the ideas in this book came out of the exchanges among the 15 or so members of the team. The point of this clarification is not to exploit their names, but rather to explain as clearly as possible the production conditions under which the interviews were done – often in English and then translated into Spanish – and above all, to honor Avi for being an extraordinary interviewer. It was surprising to watch how, despite the language barrier, his sensitivity and charisma brought out the best in every interviewee. His way of smiling and nodding at each answer could soften anybody up – even the "bad guys" in the film. Both Naomi and Avi have shown that if you know how to listen, you can understand a reality that seems distant and foreign. And in a country like Argentina, where everyone likes to talk, listening is not as simple as it sounds.

1.3 Structure of the book

To develop the subject as well as possible, and to facilitate the understanding of a phenomenon with many facets, this book is structured to present a partial but representative view. First, as we have seen, there is an overview of the topic and the decision to adopt a multi-disciplinary perspective, followed by an explanation of the conditions of production of this book, and finally, this summary of what the reader will find on the following pages.

Once this basis is established, we'll move on to the second part. The first chapter provides some background on worker control at different points and places throughout history. The goal here is simply to give the reader some idea where to look for parallels that are beyond the scope of this book. This will also provide a better understanding of the novel idea of worker control as the ultimate goal of worker struggle.

The next chapter talks about the first moments and early growth of what would become a broader movement. This section includes data on the two most institutionalized currents of the phenomenon: the National Movement of Factories Recovered by Workers (NMFRW), led by Luis Caro, and the NMRB, whose president is Eduardo Murúa. The choice of these two currents and their leaders doesn't mean they're in charge of the movement, but rather that they've participated in so many struggles that they're probably the two people with the most on-the-ground experience. That's why a lengthy interview with each is included (in the case of Murúa, lawyer Diego Kravetz[9] was also there), with the objective of getting their perspective on the phenomenon and their role in it. In the next section, questions that were hinted at in the first section are discussed in more depth, with special attention given to some of the social, economic and legal implications of this phenomenon.

First, we'll look at it from a social point of view, and try to describe it where it has the greatest power and highest hopes for growth: in everyday practice. The central hypothesis of the chapter is that the dynamic in which the workers live is a moving target, and that it moves them – if not always smoothly – towards a class consciousness (loosely defined) that most of them didn't have before. The workers' assemblies, the growing awareness of their decision-making ability, the awakening of creativity at the service of work, participation – all the things businesspeople dream about their employees doing – really do happen. Not when company communication consists of empty slogans, but rather when the workers have real and unlimited participation in decision-making.

The next subject will be legal considerations, a highly complex field for a neophyte, but one that proves decisive when the time comes to formalize a successful factory occupation. The intention is for this chapter to be a sort of introduction to the legal steps to follow and the choices the workers face in their struggle. However, it's ultimately an open question that only the workers themselves can answer in their particular case. The basic hypothesis that runs through this chapter is that the law can't respond to a new social reality with tools that have long since been left behind by practice and social necessity. It's even less able to give satisfactory answers without profound changes in legislation. The law can be considered the institutionalization of an arrangement of forces used to legitimize the status quo. In Argentina, the rule of law has been overtaken by reality. In this context, recovered factories use the law in a particular way to reach a socially necessary goal – namely, work.

When it comes to economics, the intent is to show that businesses in the hands of the workers are far from being doomed to fail, as certain businesspeople, journalists, and "common sense" gurus have repeatedly postulated. On the contrary, these enterprises have several advantages over old-style management. In the first place, the workers' commitment is different. They no longer work for the benefit of their boss – now they control the fruits of their labor. In some cases, this can lead to a more relaxed and healthier attitude toward work, but even if that happens, each worker's effectiveness still improves. No longer do they take unnecessary sick days,

---

[9]   Dr. Diego Kravetz was also elected to the legislature in the election held on 7/24/03, just as the final version of this book was being finished.

or exaggerate accidents, or goof off when the foreman isn't looking. On the contrary, they make more efficient use of materials they themselves decided to buy, and more humane use of the work day, because they know better than anyone the importance and cost of each hour.

You don't need to be a romantic to believe in this. In each factory, you can see the pride the workers take in doing the jobs for which they fought so hard. Above all, worker-run businesses are more efficient because one ingredient has been taken out of the mix: the owner cost. The pressure on the owner to make a profit at all costs (even pushing the business into bankruptcy), can manifest itself as an obstacle to the success of the business. Now, in contrast, that profit might not be there, or it might be re-invested, directed to social causes, divided up among the workers, or whatever is decided in the assembly.

Finally, it should be clarified that the primary goal of workers in control of their jobs is not necessarily economic. In other words, if productivity falls at some point but the quality of the work and the quality of life of the workers improves, they come out ahead, because that's how they've chosen to enjoy their work. It is revolutionary and qualitatively innovative for a factory to have other criteria that challenge efficiency and productivity for supremacy, even though the business still depends on them for survival. In the third part of the book, five individual cases are analyzed.[10] We try to keep the information as raw as possible, so each reader can divine their own observations, either with the tools provided in the previous section or under any other set of criteria they may choose. In none of the cases has there been an attempt to compile all the information (which would be impossible anyway). Rather, the idea is to pull out whatever is most distinctive about each factory: an especially good interview, an experience from the struggle, a failure, or the details of a worker's day in a given factory. The results may be somewhat arbitrary, but the intent is to provide details on what it's like to live through these experiences without belaboring repeated themes. The cases that have been selected are Zanón, the Chilavert Cooperative, the Unión y Fuerza Cooperative, Brukman, and the Comunications Institute Cooperative.

So, I invite the reader to plunge into this new understanding of work, which is built on the ruins of prejudice, and which opens up hope for change from the very roots of society: the productive forces. It would be dangerous, however, to fall into a romantic view that ignores the existing limitations. Beyond the stories in here, there is enough material and enough viewpoints out there for readers to find a wealth of information and valuable frameworks that escaped this researcher. Anyway, I hope you enjoy the journey.

---

[10] Editor's note: Not available for the English version.

2. The Global View

The nature of worker control is invariably a product of its historical context. Obviously, no other case has shown as clearly as this one the need for a viable alternative to neoliberalism and its panorama of desolation. That said, it's still interesting to look at other contexts and see how other workers were able to close the supposedly unbridgeable gap between the workforce and the ownership of the means of production. This book doesn't touch on the numerous theories about the pros and cons of self-organized production systems, because they're often specific to political assumptions or contexts.

2.1 Other occupied factories

There are many examples of workers who, for one reason or another, have come together to produce goods or provide services. The most daring researchers have reported on proto-cooperatives in ancient Egypt around 2500 BC, and Phoenician cooperatives involving naval insurance in the 15th century BC.[11] To avoid making a long list of historical accidents with some connection to worker control, we'll just look at examples that have existed within capitalism. The following cases are briefly laid out within the framework of recent history.

In 1760, at the same time capitalism was first being heralded, in the shipyards of Woolwich and Chatham, England, a cooperative bakery formed to produce bread the workers' families could afford. This was a threat to the millers' and bakers' monopolies, and the co-op mill ended up being burned down.

The first consumer co-ops date from the same time – such as the one formed in 1769 in Fenwich, Scotland, to try to get better prices for

---

[11] Gil de Vicente, Iñaqui, 2002.

consumer goods. This has been repeated in various countries at various times, such as the neighborhood assemblies formed in Buenos Aires at the beginning of the 21st century.

The first significant case of worker control is the series of experiments by the Welshman Richard Owen (1771-1858). After several entrepreneurial experiments into which he mixed his philanthropic ideas (he created England's first kindergarten in New Lanark), Owen published the first of four books explaining his ideas, *A New Vision of Society*. His main argument was that a person's character is primarily formed by his/her circumstances, so if a person is surrounded by appropriate influences from a young age, he or she would turn out healthy and responsible. His set-up in New Lanark, which functioned as a test tube for his ideas, became an obligatory stop for social scholars of the time. Thus, he became one of the precursors of socialism and the cooperative movement.

He proposed that the governing class establish villages of 500 hectares with 1200 people. They would all live in one big, square building with public kitchens and a playroom for the smallest ones. Each family would have their own private room and take care of their own children until the age of three, when the community would assume responsibility for their education. Owen's rejection of any kind of religion alienated him from spheres of political power, and he went into exile in 1825, purchasing 12,000 hectares of land in Indiana, USA. There, he founded New Harmony, a community that seemed to fulfill all his expectations for a while, until internal disagreements about religion and how the community should be governed arose. In 1828, he abandoned New Harmony, visiting various Owenist communities until finally deciding to dedicate his life to spreading his ideas.

Owen's ideas were more successful than his experiments. In 1824, the London Cooperative Society was formed, followed by the Brighton Cooperative Society in 1827, and in 1829, the *British Cooperator*, a newspaper devoted to spreading his ideas. By 1830, there were between 300 and 500 cooperatives. That year, Owen founded the "National Workers Fair Exchange," which used a currency based on time invested in the production of goods and included the cost of equipment and material used (accumulated work). Initially, the currency was a success, but in 1832, it failed after a violent repression of the most radical English workers, which ended with hangings and deportations. The struggle was carried on through 1838 by the first Chartist movements, which demanded electoral reform. The charter was drawn up by William Lovett, a follower of Owen.

As a result of this movement, thinkers (later considered to be pre-Marxists) such as William Thompson emerged, urging unions to form cooperatives with a communal lifestyle. According to him, workers should be co-owners, co-producers and co-habitants, exchanging goods with each other in the same way that some projects in Argentina – for example striker markets, barter networks for alternative producers, etc. – propose to do.

> Instead of vainly searching the world for external markets that are overburdened or flooded by the constant competition of starving producers, let us create a voluntary association of the working classes. They are numerous enough to assure a direct, mutual marketplace for food, clothing, furniture, and housing.[12]

Meanwhile, in France, Francois Marie Charles Fourier (1772-1837) began his "phalansteries" – agricultural cooperatives responsible for social welfare, which included rotating roles among their members. These *phalansteries* introduced themselves into both capitalist and monarchical systems of government and demonstrated a greater degree of social justice. Each member received a share of the total production of the cooperative.

One of the most interesting stories of modern worker control is the case of the weavers of Rochdale, a poor neighborhood of Manchester, England. This movement produced the Seven Principles of Rochdale that

> ... would henceforth characterize the spirit of official, cross-class, apolitical cooperativism: open membership, political neutrality, one member one vote, limited interest on capital, cash sales, profits returned to members, education and training.[13]

In general, these forms of cooperativism were a legal alternative to the more radical workers' movements arriving on the scene in Europe, particularly in times of economic crisis. That's probably why the cooperative movement gained the support of European leaders such as Napoleon III, for example, who extended certain rights to cooperative workers and supported a legal charter in 1867.

The experience most like Argentina's, including the abandonment of factories during great economic crisis, was perhaps the Paris Commune of 1871. Following France's defeat by Prussia, the wealthy (including the owners of the means of production) fled Paris. The remaining inhabitants of the city declared it a republic and tried to resist the invaders. In the short time they were able to do so, unprecedented social experiments were carried out. It was decided to leave the abandoned factories in the hands of their workers. On April 16, 1871, the Commune issued a decree:

> The Paris Commune, considering that a great number of factories have been abandoned by their directors, who have fled their responsibilities as citizens with no concern for their workers; considering that, as a result of this cowardly flight, much work of importance to community life has been interrupted, and that the lives of the workers is at stake, decrees:

---

[12] Cited in Gil de Vicente, Iñaqui, 2002.
[13] Ibid.

A convocation of workers' organizations is called to to designate an investigatory commission whose task will be:

1. To establish a count of the abandoned factories, as well as an exact inventory of the state of the factories and any equipment that may be in them;
2. To draw up a report on the conditions so that the factories can return to production immediately, not under the deserters who abandoned them but under cooperative association of the workers of these factories;
3. To create a plan for the formation of these cooperative workers associations.[14]

In 1875, the cooperative movement, based on the seven Rochdale principles, arrived in Montevideo, "where it is seen by the bourgeoisie as an element of bitter class struggle, after the grueling strike by 500 spaghetti factory workers in 1884. In 1897, an agricultural cooperative is established in Avellaneda, Argentina."[15]

Throughout the 20th century, there were a number of cases of worker control that deserve mention. One is Yugoslavia, where the government arranged for worker control of production. This was possible thanks to the ability of President Josip Broz, known as "Tito," to remain independent of Stalin's regime, which allowed him to maneuver in a way that other communist countries could not. The U.S. thinker James Petras distinguishes three stages in worker control in Tito's Yugoslavia: from 1950 to 1964, he finds there was worker control in every factory supervised by the Communist Party. From 1965 until the disintegration of the Yugoslav Federation in 1972, the factories underwent "market reform," and "began to be affected by capitalist pressures, with greater social inequities emerging among factories and economic sectors as well as unemployment."[16] After 1973, factories under worker control begin to disappear in the face of international competition, internal struggles and the problems of the Communist Party. According to two scholars who have studied worker self-management (Doctor of Sociology James Petra and the sociologist Henry Veltmeyer), its 25 years of success is fundamentally due to

...the struggle of the masses who preceded the emergence of worker self-management during the anti-fascist and anti-Stalinist periods, who mobilized and politicized the working class and promoted class consciousness and organization.

Closer to home, the Bolivian National Revolution occurred in 1952. Its greatest achievements took place during the presidency of Victor Paz Estenssoro of the National Revolutionary Movement, thanks to the support of the miners and *campesinos*. In October 1952, the three most important

---

14 Mandel, Ernst, 1973.
15 Gil de Vicente, Iñaqui, 2002.
16 Petras, James and Veltmeyer, Henry, 2002.

tin companies were nationalized, but control did not end up in the workers' hands. According to Petras and Veltmeyer's conclusions, the effects of
State control were limited by the lack of alliances with other social sectors
and similar experiences outside of mining.

In Peru, in 1968, a military *junta* under General Velasco Alvarado took
power. The nationalization of the International Petroleum Company, and of
a chemical and paper plant called Paramonga that belonged to U.S. capitalists, brought about severe international isolation. The *junta* found support
among the *campesinos* when it expropriated land to be worked by indigenous
communes, *campesino* collectives or individuals – though it was always under control of the military. The lack of any real democracy in the factories
caused the workers to stage numerous strikes against the businesses they
supposedly managed. According to Petras and Veltmeyer, "The lesson of
Peru is that expropriations or nationalization from above reproduces the hierarchical structure of capitalism and marginalize public sector workers."[17]

Another interesting case is Chile under the socialist government of
Salvador Allende between 1970 and 1973, when he was overthrown by
Augusto Pinochet. During his government, there were many expropriations[18] and some 125 factories operated under worker control. These factories were operated by "commissions of workers and functionaries."[19] In
this case, according to Petras and Veltmeyer, the very expansion of the
phenomenon caused an explosion of resistance to the threat: "The dis-
placed capitalist class resorted to violence and repression in order to regain
control of the means of production."[20]

During the strikes that accompanied the mass movement in France, in
May of '68, factories were occupied and, in some cases, began to operate under self-management.[21] There were many more such cases in countries under Communist control (for example, Czechoslovakia, beginning in 1966),
although most failed to redistribute political power. Instead, power was concentrated in a pyramid, just as it had been under capitalism, and it ended up
alienating the very workers who were supposed to benefit from it.

While there are more examples (such as Portugal in 1974), we'll stop
our review here and draw up a brief historical balance sheet. In the 20th
century, the significance and achievements of worker control or nationalization seem to be limited for a number of reasons. There were certainly

---

[17] Petras, James y Veltmeyer, Henry, 2002, p. 58.
[18] One of the most famous nationalizations – and most consequential for Chilean politics – was
that of the copper mines belonging to US interests. No indemnity was paid, because it was
decided that the profits made off the mines were more than sufficient.
[19] Petras, James and Veltmeyer, Henry, 2002.
[20] Ibid.
[21] One of the most successful cases was a high-tech company called LIP, which made watches,
tool-making machinery, and armaments, and which was under worker control from 1973-74.

cases that were exceptions to the capitalist system, but the workers were controlled from above by military bureaucrats or the Communist Party, and had little or no autonomy to make decisions. In these cases, the State played a major role in promoting cooperativism. As we'll see, the Argentine case is quite different, particularly because the initiative arose in a power vacuum, and because it's the workers themselves in different factories who decide to take action. In Argentina, the State plays an erratic role, ranging from bewilderment to consent to repression.

The closest case to us in time, space, and methodology is what's happening in Brazil, particularly since the foundation of the National Association of Workers of Self-Managed Businesses (ANTEAG), which came about in response to a series of bankruptcies in the wake of the neo-liberal experiments on our continent.

The first experience in Brazil was in 1991, when the Makerly Shoe Factory went bankrupt, leaving 500 employees suddenly without work. Realizing how difficult it would be for those unemployed workers to find new jobs, the Footwear Workers Union of the region of Franca, where the factory is located, began to look for alternatives to total closure of the factory. They were able to negotiate its purchase as a cooperative through a govern-ment loan. Unfortunately, the new self-managed business maintained a hi-erarchical structure, lacked transparency and was generally unable to create a management system that would allow the factory to grow. It finally closed its doors in 1994. Nonetheless, that same year, based on the experience at Makerly, a group of technical workers at the Inter-Union Department of Statistics and Socioeconomic Studies (DIESSE), together with the Chemists Union, decided to create ANTEAG to provide support to new self-man-agement initiatives, which tend to be similar to the recovered businesses in Argentina. The main difference is that in Brazil, the usual method is not State expropriation. Rather, the former employees buy the business from the owners using accumulated debts or, when the business comes up for auc-tion, bidding with government credits. They have a bit of extra security in that the State itself has been taking on these businesses as its suppliers.

This methodology had saved some 30,000 jobs by the middle of 2003. About 300 businesses were recovered, about half of which are members of ANTEAG. Just as in Argentina, most of these cases are not strongly ideo-logical; rather, they arose out of extreme need. One of the coordinators of ANTEAG explained to Indymedia Brazil that

> When there is no alternative and the workers run the risk of losing their jobs, the union contacts ANTEAG, and we help the employees negotiate with owners on the sale of machinery or ways jobs can be kept.[22]

---

[22] Indymedia Brasil, http://brasil.indymedia.org/pt/blue/2003/07/257665.shtml, 7/1/2003.

2.1.1 The Argentine background

It's difficult to find strong parallels between the experiences of worker control in the past and those of the last two or three years. Throughout the rich history of working-class struggle in Argentina, there have been workplace occupations with demands that had little to do with today's goal of worker control. Finding parallels with the (mostly agricultural) cooperative movement of the late 19th century would be contrived. According to a 2002 report by the National Institute of Economic Solidarity, there were 15,887 cooperatives in Argentina, and almost 30% of the population belongs to some sort of cooperative, though most of these have structures and histories that are totally different from the recovered businesses of the last few years. Most of these businesses took the legal form of cooperatives out of practical considerations, though each has its own idiosyncrasies.

During Peron's government, there was something of a boom in the cooperative movement, but the levels of worker control were much lower than in the recovered businesses. A study that tracked the historical continuity of the today's processes explained

> we want to clarify that, thus far in our historical review, we have not found any [analogous] experiences prior to 1959, which is not to say that none existed.[23]

In any case, the very difficulty in finding any historical precedents would seem to indicate that, if they did exist, they were marginal and had little real impact – as opposed to what's happening now. According to the study mentioned above, there is some precedent for factory occupations in union struggles, particularly of the *Peronistas*.

The case of the Lisandro de la Torre meatpacking plant happened after the revolution of 1955, as part of the *Peronista* resistance. This particular plant was occupied in 1958. The decision came from the new leadership of the Meatpackers Union, which was strongly linked to the *Peronistas* and had the support of the plant's neighbors, since their fate was tied to that of the workers. The occupation was triggered by the passage of a law that allowed the privatization of the Municipal Meat Market. After fruitless attempts to negotiate with the government and the emergence of internal divisions within the union, the occupation was brutally repressed, the packing plant was returned to private ownership, and 2000 workers were fired.

In 1964, during the weak presidency of Humberto Illia, the CGT drew up a plan to change government policy on a wide range of matters: freedom for all political prisoners, repeal of all repressive legislation, maintenance of jobs and creation of new ones, defense of the nation's

---

[23] Allegrone, Verónica et al., 7/8/2003.

heritage, etc. After failing to get a satisfactory response, the CGT launched the second part of its plan, which consisted of the occupation of factories for brief periods (less than 24 hours) throughout the country. Waves of partial and total occupations began in May, reaching several hundred factories each time. The last wave of occupations, in July 1964, took place in 3,400 businesses.[24] Almost 50% of the occupations were in metallurgical and textile factories. "[A]fter the second stage of the plan, the Minimum Living Wage Law was ratified, and the "independents" left the leadership of the CGT, further strengthening Vandor's position."[25] Apart from a few brief, marginal cases, the workers did not operate factories under their control.

In June of 1973, during Héctor Cámpora's brief presidency, there were 2000 occupations – not only in factories, but also in universities, hospitals, television stations, etc. This conflict was resolved through an agreement between Juan Domingo Perón, the unions, and the business leaders, but after the death of General Perón, it happened again during the government of María Estela Martínez de Perón. At that time, some sectors became radicalized as a result of the divisions within *Peronismo*. In this final stage of the movement, the workers occupied the Mancuso-Rossi paper plant and managed to set up a sort of worker control over the employers. There were some other cases of direct worker control, such as PASA Petrochemicals in Gran Rosario, but that didn't last long either.

The last case we'll examine in this section is the occupation of the Ford factory in 1985 (since later events can be considered direct forerunners to factory recovery as we now know it). The occupation of the Pacheco plant came as a response to 33 firings. Hundreds of workers gathered and decided to demonstrate their ability to operate the factory. This lasted for 18 days, at which point the Alfonsín government, the employers and a part of SMATA (the automotive union) agreed to repress and expel the workers. In spite of its limitations, this fight had an important impact because of the nature of the factory, the number of workers involved in the takeover, and because it happened relatively recently – in the period of democracy in Argentina.

As you can see, the goal in these cases was a change in the balance of power between workers and owners to enforce gains that labor had won earlier, or to push for certain State policies. None of them had the goal of restructuring the way work is organized to bring about worker self-management. In the cases where that did happen, it was to pressure the employer on certain objectives, not to demonstrate that they didn't want the employer back at all. It's also worth pointing out that a drawn-

---

24 Ibid.
25 Ibid.

out conflict takes a higher toll on the workers than on the employers or the politicians, who are better-equipped to hold out. This is an important lesson: workers in re-claimed factories should pay special attention to their economic strength.

2.2 In a crisis context

The recent rise in factory occupations is made possible by a context that legitimizes this kind of behavior socially, politically and economically. The time period that saw the growth in creativity and capacity for struggle in the working class is the same one that saw the deepening of the economic crisis that began in 1998.

Since then, the struggles at Yaguané and IMPA (each in its own way) allowed the workers to keep their jobs, although they had to take on millions of pesos worth of pre-existing debts. In the former case, the debt was owed to the previous owners, and in the latter, the debt was negotiated by the leadership of the cooperative. However, the most successful model so far appeared in 2000, when a judgment awarded the use of a metallurgical plant to the Unión y Fuerza Cooperative, which was made up of its workers. The debts of the previous owner were part of the bankruptcy case, but the workers will have to pay the costs of the expropriation proceedings (after three years, they now have this money, as we will see). This factory and its methodology served as a model (with countless variations) for many that came later, or even for some that came sooner, such as Yaguané, which only got its formal expropriation years after it started working. But, let's not get ahead of ourselves. For now, we'll examine the context in which this process occurred.

After Carlos Menem's withdrawal and his boycott of potential successor Eduardo Duhalde in the elections of 1999, Fernando De la Rúa took the reins of government. Despite some hopeful appearances, it didn't take him long to demonstrate that he was no alternative to the neoliberal model that had plunged the country into an unprecedented crisis. The number of books written about this period excuses this writer from having to give a detailed analysis of the topic, but just the same, it might be useful to look at some figures from the National Institute of Statistics and Census. They can give us an idea of the scope of the economic crisis:

In October of 2000, unemployment reached 14.7% of the able-bodied population and underemployment was 14.6%. By the middle of October of the following year, the results were 18.3% and 16.3%. Only six months later, they were 21.5% and 18.6%, respectively.

In October of 2002, the poorest 10% of the population received 1.4% of all income and the richest 10% received 37.4%.

From May 2001 to October 2002, the percentage of Argentines living below the poverty level rose from 35.9% to 61.3%, while those living in indigence rose from 11.6% to 29.7%.

Economic activity compared to the same month of the previous year dropped in almost every month from October 1998 to November 2002.

The real impact of the economic crisis can be seen in some more everyday examples: the number of urban railway tickets sold in October of 1997 was 42,194, but dropped to 26,196 in February of 2002 – only 62% of the sales of five years earlier. This means that only a little over half the people who were taking the train in 1997 were still doing so in 2002. In June of 2003, after a few months of improvement in the general economic situation, 31,141 train tickets were sold, or 73% of the number sold six years earlier.

Even before the beginning of the most severe period of crisis, the number of preventive bankruptcy proceedings increased. To better understand the picture outlined below, we must remember that in February of 2002, law 25.563 suspended execution of bankruptcy for 180 days. That's why the executive judgments and preventive and decreed bankruptcies stopped increasing the way they had over the previous years.

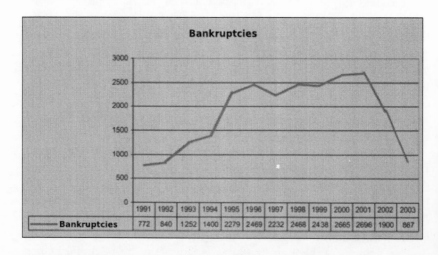

Bankruptcies	1991	1992	1993	1994	1995	1996	1997	1998	1999	2000	2001	2002	2003
Bankruptcies	772	840	1252	1400	2279	2469	2232	2468	2438	2665	2696	1900	867

The economic crisis was the result of a savage neoliberal policy that functioned as a business for international lenders and managers, generally of banks. There is endless evidence that the crisis wasn't bad for everyone; there were those who benefited from it in this country, and especially outside of it. It's not necessary to get into this too deeply; we'll just quote an article from the *Washington Post*, which belongs to a country that never accepts blame. According to the article, between 1991 and 2001, the biggest financial firms in the world brought in "about 1 billion dollars."[26] This is the flip side of the scenario presented by the statistics cited above, and also largely the reason for them. The article also explained that Wall Street was one of the accomplices in the debacle that turned Argentina from a "fantasy land" into a "catastrophe."

The economic debacle set off a chain reaction that became a seemingly terminal crisis in politics as well. It exploded in the *cacerolazos* [demonstrations of people banging pots and pans] on December 19 and 20, 2001. That's when De la Rúa's government ended, leaving a vacuum that would be hard to fill. Society suffered the impact, and a series of presidents were forced out by the population's widespread rejection of the entire political class, which was summed up in the slogan "*Que se vayan todos*," or "Out with all of them!" That cry awakened Argentine society from the consumerist stupor imposed by neoliberalism and represented by Menem.

This awakening led to an attempt to develop alternatives instead of waiting for solutions from the government. As José Abelli of the NMRB explains, the only alternative that the Argentine governing class could offer was:

> Sell everything to Petrobrás, surrender the national heritage. This Argentine establishment is pathetic. They were like the people dancing on the Titanic as it sank, the way they were asking for flexibility and complaining of the labor costs in Argentina. But the only cost here is the owner. One hundred and thirty-five billion dollars have gone up in smoke. If we seriously want to see development in this country, we will have to be part of it ourselves.[27]

As an apparent impact of the *cacerolazos*, the repression and the deaths did not last long, though all the real consequences will only be visible several years from now. Today there is still debate about whether the people brought the president down, whether it was a plot by the opposition, or whether he fell by himself. It was probably a mixture of all three.

With this power vacuum and the lack of legitimacy of politicians and business leaders, people took to the streets in a frenzy, looking for anything that would give them a sense of control over their own destiny. This political hyperactivity allowed for many new political practices, (like neighborhood assemblies), while others that already existed (like picket lines and recovered factories) grew and found more support.

Although a great deal more could be said about this period, there is an excellent and endless bibliography analyzing the crisis. We will only look at some of the data in a broader context to give a better insight into the recovered factories.

---

[26] Blustein, Paul, Washington Post, "Argentina didn't fall on its own," 3/8/03.
[27] Website lavaca.org: http://www.lavaca.org/notas/nota340.shtml, "El otro fondo".

First, we must emphasize the vacuum of political legitimacy and the sense that only grassroots organization could stop the roller coaster. This created a new social climate, which provided support for new forms of social organization, including the recovered factories. According to Cándido's experience with the Chilavert Cooperative, where the struggle took place mostly in the months after the *cacerolazos*, one of the reasons the recovered factories could exist and grow as the support of the people:

> It's not like it was before – "don't get involved." People participate. Look at us here [at Chilavert]. If it was just us, they would have kicked us out ten times over, but it wasn't just us. It was people from the assemblies, retired folks, neighbors. People are getting involved because [the system] is rotten. One way or another, everybody's been hurt by this shitty system, so it's the people who want to change it – not some know-it-all or anything like that. We're on the front line, but the the people are with us – otherwise, we couldn't keep going. Even when they don't intervene, just for them to come by and say "hello" means there's been a change in society. The change is coming from the bottom up, not from above, which would be faster. Since it comes from below, it's slower, but it has the backing of the better part of society.[28]

For many occupations that ended up succeeding, the neighborhood assemblies were important factors, both logistically and morally, because they provided support to keep up the fight against larger forces – usually in the form of court representatives, judges or the boys in blue. Chilavert was supported by the Assembly of Pompeya, El Aguante by the Assembly of Carapachay, and Nueva Esperanza (formerly Grissinopoli), Crometal, the BAUEN Hotel, and others were supported by several assemblies at once.

This help was paid back in various ways, especially in the cases where the factory stabilized: with cultural centers (Nueva Esperanza, IMPA, Yaguané, Mercado de Tigre), health centers (IMPA, Chilavert); in other cases, courses are offered (Chilavert, Veytes), school visits are arranged (FORJA San Martín, Zanón), and donations and loans are provided (Brukman, Zanón, Unión y Fuerza, IMPA).[29]

While it's a bit early to draw sweeping conclusions, you can see a correlation between the degree of aid received by the factories during the struggle and their commitment to the community and other factories. In other words, those who formed bonds in their moments of greatest weakness felt obliged to make good on them when they were strong.

Many of the new endeavors adopted an ideology similar to that of anti-capitalist organizations that strive for a horizontal decision-making

---

[28] "*Ocupar, Resistir, Producir*" magazine, MNER, N° 1, 30/11/02.

[29] The examples given represent a small number of business, because many operate on a very small scale, relating directly with their neighbors, and not much further. You have to visit them to see what they're doing beyond what they produce at the plant.

structure, usually in the form of assemblies. The objective of such structures is to avoid a pyramidal structure in which power is appropriated and used by the upper tiers for their own benefit. This new type of organization is radically opposed to the structures promoted in Argentina from Peron's time, through the dictatorship, up to the individualist neoliberalism of the 90s. It represents not only a political challenge, but also social, cultural, and even psychological. Only the deep vacuum of legitimacy left by the previous systems could allow people to break with such deeply-established structures, leading to a traumatic sense of uncertainty and personal responsibility. This vacuum is reflected in brief analyses of the recovered factories:

> The takeover of Brukman occurred in the context of the social explosion that brought down the De la Rúa government and a population that was breaking out of years of individual isolation to claim a new form of democratic participation. [...] This large-scale rupture encouraged the Brukman workers to push it even deeper, once they saw they had the support of a mobilized underclass.[30]

Analysts generally agree on the fundamental importance of the political environment to the growth of the movement of occupied businesses:

> The visibility of the movement is new, and strongly linked to the period of institutional crisis in December 2001.[31]

Other, more institutional actors on this stage, who depended on the existing structures for their survival – many of the unions, for example – were perplexed by a movement of individuals who had been passive for so many years. For example:

> The Bonaerense Federation of Graphics Workers (during the recovery of the Chilavert printing plant), the Textile Workers Union (at the Brukman factory), and the Union of Food Industry Workers (in Grissinópoli) all abandoned their members to their fate and pulled their lawyers out when the workers decided to occupy their respective factories.[32]

There are many cases of this. Workers tell us that the union promised to be there but rarely showed up, and when it did, it would would bring a box of food and a suggestion to negotiate for fewer layoffs and a reduction in the debt they were owed. There were also exceptions, as we'll see. Anyway, it's clear that, thanks to a sea change in the social climate, not

---

[30] Chaves, María, et al., 2002.
[31] Palomino, H. et al., 1/2003.
[32] Ibid.

only did new re-claimed factories emerge, but also others that had previously been hidden became visible.

Secondly, the crisis had the effect of provoking a thorough critique of the market-driven economic path the country had been following. State-owned enterprises were privatized throughout the '90s to finance a field day of consumption that came to an end when the money ran out and the bubble burst. What's more, the privatized companies proved to be just as inefficient and costly as the State companies, and even more voracious. The icing on the cake was the convertibility law, which allowed the owners to make huge profits by trading US dollars and Argentine pesos at a ratio of one to one. The public indignation at this plunder further convinced people that, just as in politics, only the citizens themselves could solve their problems, including economic ones. What's more, the economic crisis left many people with nothing to lose, ready to try anything to keep from falling out of the social system entirely. That explains why at most of the factories, the ones that saw the struggle through were the older workers, since they were the least likely to find work elsewhere. The younger ones, faced with the dilemma, preferred to go out and try to get another job, improbable as that might be. I must emphasize that while the context supported taking steps as drastic as taking over the means of production, the workers faced countless economic, legal, cultural, and even moral barriers. This took a huge toll on them, which is why they needed extra support to make their decision.

Thirdly, the end of the convertibility law, which had choked Argentine producers, gave a certain economic viability to local producers, and therefore to the recovered businesses. In the worst of the crisis,

> What used to be the exception now appears to be the rule. The bosses flee the factories. No one is prepared to come along and take their place. In the handful of cases where an interested capitalist does appear, the operation is nothing more than a front for a real estate business or speculation, or a brutal rationalization project.[33]

In other words, producing in this country wasn't seen as attractive. As we'll see, a business owner's need to make a profit is much greater than that of the workers, for whom work is essentially an end in itself, independent of its benefits. In a crisis context like we had, owners did business that had little to do with producing goods, and if they didn't make a profit, there was no reason not to close their doors. Now that there is a more competitive situation, production has become beneficial again. On the one hand, this favors recovered production, but on the other hand, it reduces the number of conflicts and makes owners more resistant to giving up their factories. In other

---

[33] Heller, Pablo, April 2003, p. 60.

words, the end of the convertibility law works in favor of factories that are established, but against any that might start up in the future. However, this variable isn't the only consideration, or necessarily the determining factor.

As we analyze the economic variables that affect the recovered factories, it's important to remember that they developed within a context of terrible crisis. This helps us understand that even if the recovered factories didn't always ensure a decent salary or benefits, the advantages of self-organization were not only political but also material, since there was a better division of what little there was, and when things got better, they stayed the course of equal distribution, as we'll see in the chapter on economics. And of course, they also bid good riddance to a host of small everyday humiliations.

As I write these lines, at the end of 2003, the economy seems to be improving, though there is debate on whether this is sustainable in the medium- and long-term. There is also greater political stability, thanks to our "do-er" President [Nestor Kirchner], who's getting results in areas that were apparently off-limits for preceding administrations. (This is in spite of a public outcry over certain issues, like the ouster of certain Supreme Court Judges, or "chop shops" for stolen cars.) Kirchner's strong numbers – he had 90% approval rating at the beginning of August 2003[34] – might address the urgency of the social movements. On the other hand, it may challenge them in new ways if people go back to delegating power, which always opens the door to its abuse if the one in whom it's concentrated uses it for personal benefit and not the common good. It was a long, slow, laborious task, learning not to trust the government, and that talking to neighbors is the best way to make decisions. However, real-world political experience would seem to indicate there are few options.

2.3. The beginning

"When property becomes more important than work tools, there's a problem. They are goods to be used, not to be possessed."

Eduardo Murúa, in an interview in August 2003

Before we look back at the beginnings of the recovered factories as we know them today, we need to set some boundaries, and above all, answer the question – what is a recovered factory? It's difficult to determine which businesses or cooperatives belong to this category and which do

---

34 These numbers are from an interview with Hugo Haime, *Página/12* newspaper, 8/5/03.

not. Many factors are in play here – not just the legal aspects of how the factories came to be (by expropriation order, by a cooperative, by de facto worker control), but also cultural and social factors, such as the organizational structure, the existence and extent of hierarchy, the functioning of worker assemblies, etc. Everyone who studies this phenomenon has the same difficulty:

> How to define factories recovered by workers is a question that poses considerable difficulty, caused mainly by the very nature of the movement they belong to, which is made up of diverse groups with different orientations.[35]

Having accepted this complexity, we can set some fuzzy boundaries for the purposes of this book. The fundamental features of a recovered business, at least as it is commonly understood, are:

That the workers exercise de facto control over the factory, and that they all enjoy the same rights in the decision-making process. In most cases, apart from de facto worker control, there is a legal framework (or the workers are seeking one) that will allow the factory to operate, however precariously.

This de facto control is the product of labor disputes that resulted in either a partial desertion by the owner (removal of equipment and machinery, layoffs and de-capitalization, etc.) or a total abandonment and/or lockout. In the large majority of cases, this process implies a struggle against management, unions, the State or a combination of the three. However, there were cases in which an agreement was reached between workers and owners, and other cases in which local government and the union collaborated with the workers.

Keeping in mind that this is a rough definition, and that it takes in a wide variety of workplaces, we can count about 170 businesses that meet the criteria, and this number is growing fairly regularly. Eduardo Murúa talked to me about "more or less 170" recovered businesses in August 2003, although he admitted it was hard to pin down an exact number. There are lists on the Internet that are updated regularly, but their information is fairly uncertain.[36]

When did all this begin? That's also hard to pin down.

There are at least a couple of isolated cases around the middle of the 1980s that, as opposed to the Ford factory mentioned above, were able to return to production under worker control. One is the General Mosconi Cooperative, a metallurgical plant in Florencio Varela, where the workers got the assets as a result of a judgment against the owners for illegal

---

[35] Palomino, H. et al., 1/2003.
[36] See www.lavaca.org or www.mner.org.ar

removal of property. The second is the Adabor Cooperative, which made bottles and silos. After the employer declared bankruptcy in 1988, management transfered credit to the workers in exchange for debts. These cooperatives were the exception at the time, and they did not make use of expropriations.

Around the time of the crisis under Menem in the late '90s, there were two struggles that would lead to the phenomenon of recovered factories. Expropriation of one of them would not happen until later, when the movement became more organized and a methodology of expropriation was developed and used.

The Yaguané meatpacking plant, located in Matanza, belonged to Alberto Samid, a friend of Carlos Menem. It was one of the largest such plants in Argentina, employing 527 people. In 1996, this monster was suffering under a debt of AR$140 million that the owner could no longer hide, despite his powerful connections. He found a solution to his problems: lay off 250 employees. Faced with this threat, the workers took over the factory and created a cooperative called Cooptrafriya. To stabilize their situation, they began to negotiate with the shareholders, who were anxious to get rid of shares that represented nothing but debts. The employees were able to negotiate 56% of the total shares in exchange for taking on the debts. Later, a judge determined that, since Samid had no participation, his shares had no value whatsoever. So, the cooperative kept operating the plant, though it couldn't escape the debts of the previous owners, and even ended up paying back bills plus judgments in lawsuits brought by former employees who refused to join the cooperative. Things were not easy, and the salaries of the nearly 500 members who stuck it out amounted to just over a bag of meat per week. They went through hard times, but they were successful. The president of the cooperative, Daniel Flores, who did not have a high school diploma at that time, took courses in economics together with other members to learn to manage their business.

To bring closure to the situation, in June of 2001, the Province of Buenos Aires issued an expropriation decree (No. 12688) that took the plant away from the corporation and gave it to Cooptrafriya. For the expropriation to take effect, the co-op had to make the indemnity payment. This had not happened after two years, and the judge in charge of the bankruptcy demanded the property back.

The provincial executive finally agreed to pay the indemnity and in August of 2003, and found itself in negotiations to decide on the amount –which wasn't easy. In 1996, the company had been assessed at AR$3.2 million, and in August of 2003, Governor Felipe Solá offered AR$5 million to the bankruptcy court in indemnity for the expropriation. The trustee demanded AR$38 million, because the business had increased its capital value (thanks to all the work and the investment by the cooperative over the previous years). Victor Turquet, a member of the Yaguané Cooperative and an employee of the National Institute of Associationism and Social Economy, explains:

> The trustee set his honorarium at AR$1.5 million, and we paid him AR$660 thousand over seven years. Now he's demanding AR$38 million, because then his share will increase. This is judicial corruption with total disregard for anything else.

Judicial corruption was not all the meatpackers had to face. Over the past few years, they had invested 600,000 dollars to get the sanitary certification that would let them to export to the European Union, which they got in October of 2002. After re-opening the European market, and after preparing the first shipment to go to Hamburg, their more powerful competitors convinced the regulatory body (SENASA) to take them off the list of exporters certified to fill the Hilton Quota.[37] According to a report issued by the workers:

> The President of the Nation, with the assistance of the Secretary of Agriculture, Fishing and Food, is intervening to try to undo this injustice, which today threatens to put the 500 workers who bet on recovering Yaguané out of work.

The list of difficulties that cooperatives face is almost endless, as we'll see. Despite it all, the Yaguané workers are optimistic. Currently, the draws are between AR$450 and AR$1100, depending on the union's categories.

The other precedent that started the movement is the IMPA metallurgy plant in Almagro, in the city of Buenos Aires. The factory was founded in 1910 and nationalized in 1945. Because of a series of economic problems, it's been a cooperative since 1961. Despite organizing this way, an internal boss class formed, which managed exactly the same way as any other: they had higher salaries, they added debt to the factory, and they refused to hold general assemblies. In 1997, the most serious conflicts began when the workers started getting draws of AR$2 a day. In 1998, the workers overcame their internal divisions, and approached a lawyer, Dr. Gallardo, through whom they met Eduardo Murúa, who later became central to the MNER, as we'll see. After several meetings, the workers were able to come to an agreement on their demands, and on May 4, made a big show of asking for an assembly. At last, on the 22nd of the month, they had the assembly, and the first decision – by majority –was that Murúa could remain, in spite of resistance from the hierarchy. When the "bosses" saw they couldn't impose their will, they left. The workers were left alone.

---

[37] Editor's note: The European Union tariff quota for the importation of beef.

That's when the struggle began to reconnect the utilities and learn to run the factory without technical knowledge, which was supposedly beyond them. The challenge grew even more when, looking over the cooperative's accounting documents, they discovered a debt of AR$6 million. As of the middle of 2003, the cooperative had paid off only a part, since the terms were for ten years, with a 4-year grace period.

Currently, the factory is working at full speed. It has more than 150 workers drawing shares (which is what the money made by cooperative workers is sometimes called) of more than AR$1000 a month, and it has a cultural center that gives back to the neighborhood and simultaneously legitimizes the cooperative. At the same time, IMPA fulfills a fundamental role in the movement because it was one of the first successful cases, because of its economic stability, and because of the political commitment of a good part of its workers – above all, Eduardo Murúa, who was its coordinator general until he ran for provincial deputy in Buenos Aires in the August 2003 election.

The other case that completes this trilogy of background stories, and which served as a guide for future stories, is Unión y Fuerza, whose struggle is described in more depth below.

For now, it will do to know that the conflict was brought on by the bosses stripping the factory's assets. Subsequently, the Federation of Worker Cooperatives (FECOOTRA) of the Province of Buenos Aires, and especially one of its lawyers, Luis Caro, helped the workers get the first expropriation for this type of case in December of 2000. Being familiar with these stories, and others that come from Santa Fe (Cooptravi, Mil Hojas, Herramientas Unión), IMPA called a meeting of representatives from Rosario, FECOOTRA, Unión y Fuerza, and Yaguané in the middle of 2001.

Murúa recalls:

> We came together primarily to see how we recovered businesses could connect, and how we could give ourselves an organizational framework to put this form of worker struggle in the big picture. Out of that meeting came the idea of a movement, even though there were *compañeros* who thought we needed to form a federation. To others of us, that didn't seem right, because the businesses that made it up wouldn't necessarily have to be cooperatives, and it was more about a movement of the social economy.

After this debate, Yaguané and FECOOTRA decided to keep working on their own, and the people of Santa Fe that were with Abelli and IMPA (Murúa) created the NMRB. At first, Luis Caro would stay with the former group.

The movement started to grow in the fertile soil of bankruptcies and conflicts that grew towards December of 2001. The successful struggles began to spread by word of mouth. The factories in conflict approached the MNER, and the number of recovered establishments grew quickly. If it was the depth of the economic crisis that gave the movement strength, it was the social debacle of 2001 that paved the way towards greater social and political legitimacy. Víctor Turquet of the Yaguané cooperative remembers:

> When that hellish December came, people came to Yaguané, asking for help, and we didn't even have gas money. We couldn't deal with all that. So we set up a project to create the Executive Unit of Recovery of Businesses in Crisis, with Daniel Flores, president of the Yaguané Cooperative, Horacio Repetto, Marcela Díaz, and me. It was a project of the Yaguané Cooperative. We presented the project in INAES when Dr. Elvira Castro took charge, and by April 2002, they called us saying there was demand to learn about the subject, but there was no one who knew about it. We started up on May first.

The first work that the group formed around Yaguané did was in Santa Isabel in Santa Fe, and Avícola Moreno and Minguillón in Moreno. Soon, political differences emerged with Luis Caro that led to his departure for the MNER, where he also didn't last long, leaving in early 2003. According to Eduardo Murúa, the separation was the result of

> personality conflicts. There was a confrontation, which was sometimes childish, between Caro and Abelli for leadership. Sometimes I felt uncomfortable, because I could work well with each of the *compañeros*, but the two of them just couldn't get along.

Another source of division between these two leaders, which is more perceptible now, came from ideological differences. While Abelli and Murúa spoke out in favor of national liberation, Caro recovered jobs without providing a deeper criticism of the economic model or international power. Something of these different perspectives can be seen in the interviews below. Finally, faced with the impossibility of resolving these differences, Dr. Luis Caro formed his own force, the National Movement of Factories Recovered by the Workers (MNFRT), of which he is the president.

On this point, some clarification is needed. While the leadership of both movements and their directors is important when a factory reopens, above all because of their experience, it would be a mistake to suppose that they remain a determining influence once the workers become stabilized. When a factory is mentioned, it's common to hear "That one is Caro's," "That one is Murúa's," "That one is FECOOTRA's," but the reality on the ground in most factories is quite different.

What does it mean for a given factory to be in one movement or another? It's hard to answer, because the intrinsic distrust the workers have for anything that resembles a boss makes it difficult to do anything that would compromise their autonomy. Luis Caro has contracts with some of the factories thanks to those he charges for his legal services, in turn allowing him to organize a larger structure to support new conflicts. At the same time, some professionals close to Caro do paid work for the cooperatives, mostly in administration.

How much power this means in reality is hard to determine, as we'll see. The factories treat their autonomy as a flag that they have no intention of lowering.

The MNER, for its part, has nothing like these contracts. Some businesses (primarily IMPA), however, chip in to help meet the costs of the movement, whose members finance themselves as long as the struggle takes. According to Murúa, this economic independence

> lets the cadres discuss their policies freely. The personal autonomy of each *compañero* is fundamental to the life of the organization, so they aren't depending on some *compañero* who can get them something.

Murúa accepts that the movement has no control whatsoever over what happens inside the factories, or the extent of the help they might give when the movement needs them. Once their own conflict is over, most workers go back to a low level of combativeness.

> That's because of the conditions our people live in. We can't tell a *compañero* who hasn't taken on this struggle, and who hasn't become a political cadre, to change his whole life if all he's ever done with it is work and go home and watch Channel 9. Today, he does the same thing. We can't turn 12,000 workers into 12,000 political cadres. There are probably one or two per business that are committed to the movement and the struggle, but no more.

As for the situation of both movements as of the middle of 2003, both workers and leaders recognize that there are positive signs from the government promising to oil the machinery of factory recovery. There are hopes for modifications to the bankruptcy law, the creation of a fiduciary fund that helps with capital for the cooperatives, the possibility of debt forgiveness for workers that take over management of businesses and even the possibility of transforming some of the cooperatives into suppliers for the State. Following an agreement between the MNER and the Ministry of Labor in the middle of July 2003, Minister Carlos Tomada affirmed that there was a presidential decision to support the recovery of those businesses forced to close their doors due to the crisis of the last few years."[38] At any rate, as Murúa explained in a meeting at the beginning of August, "during these months, there were some positive signs, but nothing concrete," so we'll have to see what happens in the future.

---

[38] Press Gazette of the Ministry of Labor, 7/14/03.

During a meeting in the middle of July 2003, José Abelli synthesized the new relationship being established with the government, which shows a growing recognition of the work being done by the movement:

> We always have to remember that we got to this point because we occupy, resist, and produce. A year ago, nobody in the State paid any attention to us, and today, we're sitting down to talk directly with them. That doesn't mean we should stop mobilizing – that's our strength. Now that we have negotiators, we need to start to oil the tools that can help us. Also, it should always be clear to them and to us that they are the State and we are not, we are the workers. What we can start up for them, we will. Everything is fine as far as roles go. There seems to be political will, and supposedly there are AR$7 million for credits on excellent terms for factories that present viable plans. It remains to be seen if there will be problems with providing that money, and that's where we'll find out how much they really want to help us. I also see political will. We need to keep in mind that outside of the province [of Buenos Aires] and the capital, not only are there no negotiators, ...there aren't even expropriation laws.

Víctor Turquet, of INAES, reported that between June 2002 and May 2003 they had worked on 62 cases, but that in 2003 they saw the number of conflicts decline.

> The number of conflicts is decreasing because the country is moving, even if it's walking on its knees, crawling, or slouching. Over the last few months, the people are very slowly getting back to work. You could see it in the number of cooperatives that requested to sign up. So, what direction do we go in? Well, let's strengthen the ones we already have, let's train, let's structure. But the topic of recovered factories came back into style because the politicians needed it for their campaigns. It's not like we're trying to close our doors, but we were thinking of dedicating ourselves to strengthening what's already been built. There, this office has to work for six more months and then close.

There are a lot of enemies to face. With the improvement in the economic situation, business owners can put their capital back to work, and make the struggle for recoveries more difficult, or even offer sums of money that are irresistible to workers who are less convinced that they want to be their own bosses. This is something that already happened (as we saw) in one of the most symbolic factories of the movement in Brazil. A report from the Executive Unit of Recovery of Businesses in Crisis (INAES), which Turquet directs, concludes in an analysis of recovered food-services businesses:

> The experiences of the Vizental, Santa Elena, Avícola Moreno, and Fricader meat-packing plants show this tendency. It is the opinion of this Unit that assistance should be increased to businesses that have stabilized, to strengthen their position in the industrial sector and allow them to serve as witnesses to the social economy in areas traditionally characterized by domination by large economic groups.

Owners are not the only rising threat. Turquet insists there is one characteristic the factories need: autonomy. According to him, there are many cases where workers fight for impossible goals just to keep some partisan flag flying in front of the cameras, or are directly co-opted for someone's personal power. He assures us that efforts at INAES and Yaguané are directed at making sure the workers manage themselves in a truly autonomous way. This makes Turquet's perspective different from other businesses. You could say he's a fundamentalist of cooperativism. He believes there's a need to strictly respect cooperative doctrine and the fundamental principles of worker cooperatives: participation of everyone, democratic organization, no discrimination on the basis of ideology or political party, no exclusion of any workers who are members and finally, peaceful demands. Work should be "constructive, silent, and far from the risks of media exposure."

A document from INAES, signed by its director, Dr. Elvira Castro, criticized the use of cooperatives for political ends:

> In these cases, worker cooperatives emerged as an almost exclusive alternative, but we have noticed on several occasions that their basic outlines have not been respected. The efforts of many have been used for the benefit of a few, and this has created a pseudo-movement that has developed into something inorganic, permeable to partisan politics, and dependent on magical solutions that are not based on a real culture of work.

Even with these reservations, Turquet agrees that most factories develop an important degree of autonomy. Those that don't figure out how to shake off those seeking only their own interests don't survive. Factories where production overrides other objectives tend to fail, while those that prioritize sustainability can act politically, or not, as the assembly decides.

This has been a snapshot of the situation of the phenomenon of recovered factories, or at least its stronger tendencies. We left out particular cases with different forms of struggle or different objectives, such as Zanón or Sasetru, whose characteristics will be analyzed below. As for the future of the movement, it's best for each reader to reach the end of the book, and their own conclusions.

2.3.1 Statistics

In this section, we'll briefly analyze the quantitative characteristics of the movement. As we've said repeatedly, the recovered factories don't have a measurable impact on the national economy. Their effect on society is due more to qualitative factors than quantitative, so we won't go into much depth on this aspect.

Still, to give a tentative idea of some indicators that will provide a better idea of these characteristics, we'll look at a survey done by the MNER, which was not finished as this book was being written. Given the constant changes in the factories' individual situations, it's hard to capture any particular moment in time.

With this in mind, we present some graphs using data based on a sample of 160 factories (except where it specifically says otherwise), describing where they are, what they make, and how many workers they have.

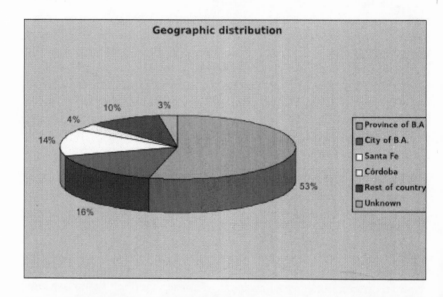

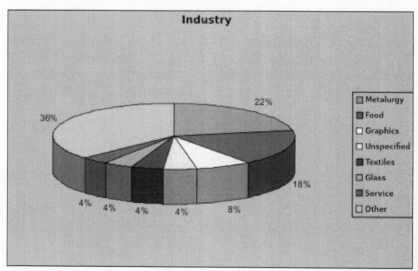

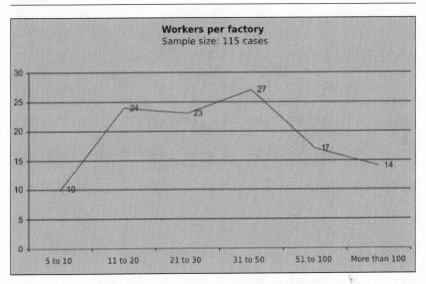

The average number of workers in a sample of 115 factories: 52. This list doesn't include La Esperanza Sugar Mill[39] in Jujuy,[40] which has 2200 employees, because it would bring the average to 71 workers per factory.

2.3.2. Two recovery movements

As I've said, to think that the recovered factories answer to a movement outside their assemblies would be to underestimate their very real autonomy. The different organizations involved in the businesses in conflict usually have an important role in the first stage of the struggle, but generally, when they reach some kind of legal stability, that role is limited to a moral commitment that does not obligate the workers in any way. There are times when the members of the movements join them to advise in administrative or legal tasks, but generally this function doesn't necessarily imply a stronger alliance with the organizations. The reality is that the limited resources of the movements, especially the MNER, as we'll see, make it hard to have a closer relationship with the workers. The workers, for their part, are committed to the difficult task of getting a factory working, which totally absorbs them, at least for the first few months, so much that they can't offer much to the movement or other factories, either in time or economic support. Besides, the experience of the struggle gives the workers a healthy distrust for any organization with a whiff of

---

[39] The plant was occupied by the workers and, as of August 2003, there was no clear decision to continue the struggle against the boss and definitively take over the factory.

[40] Editor's note: Jujuy is a province in the north of Argentina, bordering Bolivia.

institutionalism or hierarchy that might imply even the slightest level of delegation of power. There are exceptions, but as we said before, when support for such-and-such a person is privileged over the objectives of the business, that brings the price of internal conflicts and decreased efficiency, which could end up closing the business.

So, it's hard to determine the real commitment these businesses have to the various movements, and in any case, the bond is more affectionate than formal. Anyway, keeping in mind the strong autonomy of the recovered businesses, it will be useful to analyze their structures and hear the opinions of two leaders of the movements that are doing the most to help open new factories, and are probably the most involved in and knowledgeable of this phenomenon.

The National Movement of Factories Recovered by the Workers

Lawyer Luis Caro, together with the Federation of Worker Cooperatives, helped the workers of the Unión y Fuerza Cooperative achieve the first expropriation for this kind of conflict in 2000. They were still lacking some supplies when a factory in conflict called Gip Metal, S.A., approached them. This would become the basic model for other conflicts.

Caro, who has a history with the JP [*Peronista* Youth], and who, as we saw, crosses the spectrum of organizations related to recovered businesses, is the president of the one he himself created, the Movement of Businesses Recovered by the Workers (MNFRT). He has a surprising number of widely disparate contacts. Among them is the Catholic Church (he is part of the Social Pastoral Committee), and he also has good contacts in politics – his wife, Liliana de Caro, is a city council member in the legislature of Avellaneda. Caro also ran for mayor of Avellaneda at the beginning of 2003, on the later-discredited ticket of Adolfo Rodríguez Saá and Aldo Rico, even though he emphasized in several media reports that he would have liked to have been the candidate for Izquierda Unida [the United Left], with whom he also had a good relationship. He also worked with ARI. Likewise, he maintains links with various businesspeople – like the owner of the San Cayetano Supermarkets – often through having provided them with occasional legal advice. Also, he was part of the re-opening of Renacer [Rebirth] Cooperative (formerly Grundig) in Tierra del Fuego, where he was strongly supported by Corriente Clasista y Combativa [the Classist and Combative Current].

How can a man bring together such a broad range of relationships? Perhaps the best definition is the one he himself gave on lavaca.org before the presidential elections of May 2003:

I'm not an anarchist. As La Renga says, not even an anarchist. A rebel, maybe. I agree with the de-legitimization of politics, of these rulers who cost us jobs day after day. I'm going to see if they can be recovered. Not only can the social movements go a long way, but they must challenge power. Today, I have such a possibility. As a *Peronista*, you always have to be conscious of taking power. The top three candidates for the presidency are Justicialistas or pseudo-Justicialistas. To believe anything else is to fail to understand the political nature of power.[41]

Caro has created more than a few misgivings in the larger community. On the Partido Obrero's website, he was accused of a lack of solidarity with the working class, because he called the occupation of Sasetru (which the PO organized) "political."[42]

Others close to the phenomenon of the occupied factories feel he's building a very personalized sort of power, in the style of his model, Juan Domingo Perón, who he quotes constantly. He proposes to put himself in charge of solving the businesses' legal problems so they can work, and as a result, he looks like the hero of their success. This attitude leaves Zanón's much more "politicized" Raúl Godoy perplexed. In an interview, he told of his surprise at the way one of the cooperatives in the MNFRT chose to struggle:

> There was a case where we went to the cooperatives in Buenos Aires, we got to the door and tried to talk with them about certain points, and they sent us to talk to Dr. Caro, the lawyer, which came as a shock, but we understand, because the *compañeros* didn't have any previous experience.

In another factory with which Caro worked, one of the employees told us that he was among a minority in the factory each time he opposed a measure suggested by Caro. According to what I heard, the final decisions were made by the lawyer – not because he gives orders, but rather because he presents himself very humbly and feels "hurt" if anyone takes issue with his opinion. "He talks until he wears everyone out and gets what he wants," this person told me.

This kind of leadership, if it undermines the real autonomy of the workers, could represent a risk to the movement, because the workers may not learn to value themselves, and could be used for purposes that have nothing to do with them. In Caro's case, the risk that this will happen is magnified, because he's agreed to be a candidate for mayor of Avellaneda on the ticket of Adolfo Rodríguez Saá and Aldo Rico – two people who are not likely to support opening factories. In an interview with lavaca.org, he was asked, "As a militant social activist, don't you see it as contradictory to be on the ticket with Aldo Rico?" He responded,

---

[41] lavaca.org "Bosta y barro." This note predates the presidential elections of 2003.
[42] Pitrola, Néstor, "El control obrero es la política de la clase obrera", web site of the Partido Obrero, http://www.po.org.ar/ po/po798/respuest.htm, 04/14/2003.

I agree with the proposals of Rodríguez Saá and Rico. I don't see any contradictions with these people. That's the problem with the Left in Argentina – it's forever debating people, and so it splits. I'm not saying that to get politics done, you have to swallow a toad every day, but every so often, you do. The General said that politics is made with manure and mud. If you don't do that, you won't make it. The most important thing is to be clear: If I'm mayor, neither Rico nor Rodríguez Saá is going to tell me what I have to do.[43]

These are some broad strokes that give some insight into the broad gamut of personalities and motivations that intersect in the story of the recovered factories, although Caro in particular doesn't represent everyone immersed in the phenomenon, nor does he actually even carry much weight in it. In reality, if there's anything that characterizes all the variables of the recovered factories, it would be the diversity, and the difficulty of simplifying and precisely defining this diversity.

Interview of Luis Caro

This interview was conducted by Naomi Klein for the documentary we were filming. It took place at the Vieytes Cooperative (formerly Ghelco), which currently serves a base of operations for Luis Caro and the MNFRT. He was dressed sharply in a dark suit and tie. In the background, you could see machines working away, producing ice cream or maybe chocolate. Caro has a clear, calm, and convincing way of talking, and is generally agreeable to listen to. At the time we did the interview, in April 2003, signs had appeared in Avellaneda proclaiming him a candidate for mayor.

Naomi: Could you tell us where we are now?

Caro: We're in a factory that was called Ghelco. It's a factory that makes products like ice cream, candy, and desserts. February 13, 2002, the owners of the business filed for bankruptcy. The case is similar to many others in Argentina. They became indebted – to the workers, the provisional lenders, and all the creditors. This business owed around AR$20 million, so what do they do? Their maneuver was to file for bankruptcy, and then be able to buy it back through a third party, a front man, and put it back to work. As you see, this factory is in perfect condition, and it produced very well. What happened is that this process of liquidation of the liabilities, or of leaving aside the creditors through the payment of – for example, this factory is worth no less than AR$30 million, and there were offers of AR$750,000 or a million... You see what I'm saying? That was

43 lavaca. org "Bosta y barro", sitio web: http://www.lavaca.org.

the price people could pay. Suppose they could pay AR$3 million, but they were leaving out the debt from before.

Then there was discouragement in the workers, because they weren't just picking who was going to take over, but they also weren't going to pay them the money they were owed by the supposed former owner. Most of them were owed seven months of wages, two bonuses, vacations, and pension payments. In this process, the workers became financiers for the owners. Instead of getting outside credit, they just didn't pay the workers. What Argentina lived through was the discarding of work, and therefore the subject of work, which is to say, the workers. The unions couldn't do anything about it, either. A lot of the time, they had a relationship with the owners. I mean, to maintain this submissive situation.

Salaries were minimal, and retirement funds and all that simply didn't exist. So, it reached the point of bankruptcy on February 13th. As of that point, the workers started making contact with other *compañeros* in other factories, with Lavalán, which is here in Piñeyro. They called me at 12:30 at night, and the next day we met in one of their houses, and the following night, we met at 11:00 in front of the factory. What I tried to do was to make direct contact with the workers in the workplace. That's fundamental as far as I'm concerned, because the process depends greatly on the willpower and effort of the workers. I can say that I act with them in all ways – social, legal, organizational – but I know this is really their fight, and if they're not there, it's unlikely a judge or D.A. or the government itself will help. They're the basis for this.

N: What did you do before you did this full-time?

C: It's always been my conviction to change the world around me. I lived in a very poor part of Avellaneda, in pure misery.[44] I say that with great honor. Thanks to the efforts of my parents, my family, and God, I was able to study and become a naval machinist, and I sailed to different places as an officer in the merchant marine. I always had a worker's conviction that I could unite people, having long seen factories that were abandoned, rusting, with weeds growing up around them, with the workers all at home. Many times I talked with them, and they told me their factory had closed five, six, even ten years ago, and they were unable to open it. Add to that the fact that there are more than 20 million poor people in Argentina, but milk gets dumped out of its barrels. In Argentina, you could see on TV how the dairy employees dumped out milk that wasn't profitable. And because I also have a deep religious conviction, I believe

---

[44]   Editor's note: In Argentina, the poorest shanty towns are referred to as *villas miseria*. It is likely Caro refers also to this when he says he used to live in *pura miseria*.

deeply there can be another world, with more solidarity. This system is based on making a god out of money at the expense of working people.

So, I said, "I'm going to try to do what I can." The first factory was Unión y Fuerza in Avellaneda, in August of 2002, and I really didn't know what to do. I knew I had to defend the right to work, sure, I was convinced of that, and also knew we had to mobilize. I knew that mobilizing workers would change some people's minds. Several times, I had to go to interviews with really tough judges who wouldn't listen, and I introduced them to the workers, with their calloused hands, who told them, "Look, after 40 years in that factory, today, I have nothing to take home to my kids," they'd say, crying. And the judge would swallow and say, "I'll do everything I can, everything within my reach." So, that's what brought the reality of the situation home to them. Then they'd look at the machines on one side, and the workers on the other, unable to use them, and they'd say, "What's keeping you from using those machines?" Thanks to God, and a little creativity, we were able to come up with the machines, and the workers are the only ones who can run them – because you can look for some other worker, but they won't have any experience with those machines. Only the ones who worked in those factories.

N: When you saw that the closed factories weren't the end of the story, how did it change your vision of the country?

C: I always thought – I think because of my parents' influence – the more people told me the country was poor, the more I thought the country was rich. We have everything in Argentina, and I started seeing it, starting from solidarity. That's what I tell the *compañeros* in the factories: "Never break the solidarity system. The system that left you unemployed is the old one, which was selfish, materialist, and individualist. Look for another system where you, together with your *compañeros* in this, that, or the other factory can build a better world. I always tell them that, inside them, the revolution has already come, and the same thing in the factories. You used to be in a dependent relationship – you depended on someone else. And then, thanks to this whole process, you became liberated workers, individually and collectively."

So, this is something you see in the workers. It's a beautiful thing... The first days of work, they came carrying their bags, on their bicycles. Today, they're buying themselves cars and thinking about how to take their kids to school. Many of them have become tourists. Some have told me: "It's been 20 years since I've seen my mother. I'm going to see her in Corrientes."[45] That's a beautiful thing. Workers have always produced wealth, but the

---

[45] Editor's note: A province in Northeast Argentina.

thing is, they haven't gotten anything in return. Worldwide, workers get 50% of businesses' profits. In Argentina, it's no more than 5-7%. All totally because of greed. And this new system is on its way to recovering Argentina. I don't know if this is capitalism, or if it's socialism, or if it's Marxism. To me, it just means workers can have health, housing, education, recreation, and culture. This is the minimum a human being has to have.

I ask the workers why we defend the factory, even when the police come. It's very difficult to refuse to evict people from a factory when a judicial order comes down. So, why do we do it? Because in Argentina, the National Constitution says, in Article 17, that property is inviolable. And in Article 14, it says that all Argentines have the right to work and carry out any legal industry. So, these two articles are right up at the Constitutional level. And work creates dignity. The person who doesn't work is a person without dignity, like a person without freedom.

These days, we can't conceive of slaves. But before, there were those who were born slaves and died slaves; or women: they were treated like nothing more than objects. And human progress brings us to this. So, I think there will come a time when the community itself won't be able to accept there being people without work. Today, we have to fight, debate and defend it with all our conviction. The workers say it all the time: "Our feet point forward from here. Because we have to work. And if this factory gets auctioned off, we're not going to get what's ours." For example, here in Argentina, the Ministry of Labor barely exists, and it doesn't have police power, as it's called. The labor law gives rights to the workers, and the judgments are favorable to workers, but then they never see the money. That's why it occurred to me to go directly to the means of production, the machines, because anything else is in vain, it wouldn't keep people alive.

Naomi: How many factories do you work with?

In the MNFRT, there's a total of 80, and I have direct contact with 70. They all have the same system, which is based on all the decisions being made by workers' assemblies. Also, there's no manager, rather the assembly decides everything: from turning on a lamp to turning it off. What happens is that the workers delegate authority to different *compañeros*. Now, the owner's not here, he's in the assembly. The pyramid-shaped chain of command has changed, you might say.

One very important thing is that we don't accept external management. I'm convinced, as I have been from the start, that the workers can run their factories. This is one of the paradigms they're breaking with. They themselves told me: "Luis, we can't manage this factory." I told them, "Yes, you can't do it now, but nothing says you never will, if you learn." There's a worker here, Miguel, the secretary of the cooperative, who didn't know how to read and write. He operates the computer now. We taught him. They have this capacity.

Another fundamental point is that they should not depend on capital. Why didn't these processes happen before in Argentina? It was always said that you needed AR$50,000, or AR$100,000, to start producing, because you have to pay for raw materials, utilities, supplies. And I always tell them: "Guys, you can start this process. You don't need a single peso." Not for the rent contract, like in Ghelco's case, for example, or to buy raw material, either: what we do is work *a façon* [in which the client provides the raw material], and sell our labor, at first. Then we pay the electric bill, the gas bill, and other utilities at the end of the month. So, the first week, you work fast, and you get the first credit to later be able to pay for supplies. That's how you start: with zero capital. This is fairly contradictory, because we're taught that first you need to have capital to invest, to sell, to pay for everything, and then take out your profits – and if there are no profits, you reduce salaries, you suspend production, throw people out, or maybe close the factory. We manage ourselves with a different logic. That's fine, we accept that one, but it's not the only one that exists.

Why are recovered factories economic successes, and why do they enter the market? Because they fulfill two basic conditions. The interest of the merchant, as Adam Smith said, is economic. If they have quality and price, they'll sell. There's no problem whether they're workers or not. So, they have the quality. I ask them: "You're the same workers who have made this product for 20 or 30 years. Can you guarantee quality?" The price of all products includes raw materials, supplies, utilities, and taxes, and then there's the labor cost and the owner cost. The owner cost in Argentina is extremely high. Manager salaries are 10 to 20 times higher than worker salaries and utilities, something which is called surplus value. That disappears. Also, in this process, labor cost isn't a cost: it's an investment. Because they assume responsibility for not making one peso for the first months – one, or two, or three. So, the price, without labor costs or owner costs, is very good. And if the client also brings the raw material and supplies, and sometimes even fronts the money, then the process can start, because these are serious workers.

N: How sustainable is this, keeping in mind that it depends on other people's machines? The original capital was in place before the workers took it over. So, how far can this model be extended?

C: This was the problem I faced in the first factory. For example, we didn't have the machinery or the property, because they belonged to the bankruptcy case. The judge had taken them over to be able to sell them. So, it occurred to me to make an expropriation law. Private property is inviolable, but there are two ways private property can be lost. One is that a judge can rule that it must be auctioned off. The second possibility is the expropriation law – an asset is declared to be of public utility and expropriated, and the owner is paid an indemnity. So, that's what happened. I did the first expropriation of Unión y Fuerza, a cooperative in Avellaneda, to be able to use the property and its assets. We rented it, which is to say, we had a location contract. The idea was this: at first, the workers only have use, which is to say, they're not the owners. So, here's the big difference with occupying the factory without owning it. If you enter a factory, most of the time, we do it with authorization from the judge. The trustee lets us enter, and gives us the factory. This is the first stage. In the second, we use the expropriation law, which definitively settles the question of who the owner is. You pay an indemnity in return. Most of the factories are bankrupt, or closed, or the owners have abandoned them. So, Argentina is getting no benefit from them. The creditors, even less. So, what I thought was: we need to start solving problems, from small to big. I never believed that work was simply going to come along, any minute now. So, I talked to the judges to try to convince them that at a closed factory, the ravages of time take their toll, and thieves break in, and a closed factory has no value compared to a working factory.

Why did I tell them this? Because it's according to the law. I'd like to see it changed, so judges can offer a factory to the workers. I think at some point, the legislators will take this history into account and make a law. If they liquidate or sell off these bankrupt factories, a good portion of Argentine productive power will be destroyed. And not just that: we'll lose the experience the workers have acquired with these machines. A lathe can be sold as scrap iron, but for a worker, that lathe really represents work for three people: the master turner, the assistant and the laborer. This is the big contradiction. The judge has to sell it, but I think there should be a New Deal, a new contract, without forgetting about the rights of the creditors or owners. This should be a process where in about two years, the workers can have the resources to pay for the assets. At first, they aren't the owners. But they can use them, and later pay for them at a reasonable price. And I tell the workers: "You worked here for thirty years. What did you get at the end of that? Nothing. Unemployment. The truth is, I, Luis Caro, would work one year to own this factory. Don't you think that'd be good?"

N: How did you decide to run for mayor and become a politician?

C: Really, I've always been in politics. I've been active in social and political issues in Avellaneda. My wife is a city council member for the Justicialista party, and I've always been a militant as well. What happened was that two years ago, I stopped being so active, because I was busy working directly with the factories, because I'd seen that getting involved with politics didn't provide any possibility of controlling the fate of my community. I've always wanted to be where the decisions are made. In Avellaneda, there are about 350,000 people, with close to 150,000 people living in poverty, and 300 closed factories, because this was a heavily industrialized zone. Also, militants from the party asked me. There were several possible people, and they wanted me to be the candidate, because they had seen on TV and in the papers that I do what Peron once said: "To govern is to create work." The first time, I said no, I didn't want to. But they insisted, and I took the opportunity, because you need to get to where the decisions are made.

I agree with those who say out with them all, because they left Argentina in this situation. But we also need to gain experience with politics and concern ourselves with public affairs. The workers said to me, "Luis, you're going, you're leaving us!" "Just the opposite," I said. "If I win, this will be the first mayor's office with a department that specializes in recovering factories." If we can get this far by our own means, with nothing but elbow grease... I don't see any contradiction. I'm not an anarchist. I live in a democratic system where those who are morally and intellectually best qualified have to get to where decisions are made to change this world. The presidential candidate is Adolfo Rodríguez Saá, and the gubernatorial candidate is Aldo Rico. Both are very good administrators, beyond the personal issues each might have. I've always done things for Avellaneda. I'm president of an institution for the prevention of drug addiction. I was also a delegate of the Pastoral Social Committee of the bishop of Avellaneda-Lanús, where I always worked on conflictive topics. To me, it's normal to be a candidate. It's not something that contradicts my thinking.

N: Some people are worried because Aldo Rico bases his talk on the idea of security, and could target the movement, because it doesn't respect private property.

C: Well, the truth is, I haven't talked with Aldo Rico. If he's against recovered factories, that's his problem, not mine. I'm a candidate for the party that represents Rodríguez Saá and Rico, but everyone has their own thoughts. I don't think that's correct, because I established contact with him over several factories with problems in San Miguel, where he's governor. What happens is that there are a lot of situations that are managed badly. There are many situations in history where things have changed. I think if Aldo Rico and I have any disagreements, it'll be his problem. I agree that we have to preserve private property. I think it should be defended. I think it's in human nature to own things. What happens is that in Argentina, private property should be recognized, but secondary to work. Perón said it best: we need to put capital at the service of the economy, and the economy at the service of social well-being. We have things backwards here in Argentina. We have social well-being at the service of the economy, and the economy at the service of capital. I have a lot in common with Rico. He won with 70% of the votes in San Miguel. "A lot of times," Jauretche said, "the people don't know what they want, but they do know what they don't want." I understand that there are many *compañeros* on the left, in the PTS, in the Partido Obrero, in the MST, in Izquierda Unida, that criticize me. What happened is none of them said anything to me. Nobody said, "Hey, Luis, we want you to be our candidate." If Izquierda Unida had offered, I would have gone with them. But nobody offered.

N: Do you think this model could work in other countries?

C: Yes, I'm convinced. I think so, because it's based on two basic elements: machines, or tools, and workers. All over the world, there are workers who know how to do their job. All over the world, there are factories. Conditions aren't the same all over the world as they are here, but in places where there are closed factories and workers, it can happen. The question is who get the profits that are generated. What we say is that the workers should have them, and the hardest thing for any worker in the world – which I think is the same thing that happened here – is to ask: Am I trained, can I take on this commitment, can I be responsible at the end of the day for paying the utilities, paying the taxes, and dividing up the profits among my *compañeros*? And I'll tell you, those workers always took that risk. Because, in their years of work, they had to pay utilities, taxes, raw material. So, have no doubt. You can do it. You have to make an effort. You don't get anything without effort. These Ghelco workers spent more than two months with a tent at the door, protecting the assets. I think it can be done anywhere.

The Movement of Recovered Businesses

Eduardo Murúa is the current president of the MNER and, along with José Abelli and the lawyer Diego Kravetz, is the most visible head of the organization. We ran across Murúa dozens of times in different factories we visited and meetings we attended. Numerous times, we saw him explain how to recover a factory to workers who had just started considering fighting for their jobs. That's a difficult task in a country with an unemployment rate like Argentina's in the 21st century. In general, what holds the movement together is not love, but fear.

Eduardo Murúa is just over 40 years old, with a combative past and present, and a tendency to cut to the chase in any chat:

I'm a *montonero* [guerrilla fighter]. Being a *montonero* these days means doing what I do: fight to change the nation, to liberate it, and be where I should be, together with the people. Today, from this organization, the MNER, I carry out a fight that's not so much economic as symbolic, because of what it means for the recovery of businesses.

The motivation for the fights Murúa carries on is the hope of being able to awaken the conscience of the workers and make them go beyond just recovering their jobs. He accepts credit for only a meager list of achievements and admits that he still doesn't know when this fight will really take root because, as he says, political consciousness is a hard goal to reach. With a few short phrases, he painted the panorama of the movement in August 2003:

In most cases, it's not like the workers got the idea of setting up a "soviet" [workers' council] and went out and did it. It was need that pushed them and drew them into a fight that, in a lot of cases, was very important. So, you can't ask any more of these *compañeros*. Political commitment is an issue in each one of these experiences. The fight goes as far as commitment does. If we had 12,000 militants, we wouldn't be talking around this table. There's no point in getting mad at reality. Don't forget that we spend a half-hour or an hour with the *compañeros*, and they spend five or six with the enemy: television. The power of the media is very strong. That's why we have a different structure than other social organizations. We don't even insist that the *compañeros* turn out for the marches of the rest of the movement. They don't depend on handouts from us. We go out and provide serious solidarity to the workers. All we ask is that when they're doing better, they help others. Now, if they don't do it, that's their responsibility. We're not going to do anything.

Anyone who's interested can go to the MNER meetings, and more than once, I got in line without anyone asking who I was. The same thing happens with cooperative members, who go when they're interested and don't when they're not, because there's no consequences for not going. What usually happens is that those co-ops still in conflict tend to have better attendance, and those that consider themselves stronger (with some exceptions) are less militant, because they have less time or less need to fight.

Perhaps this drop-off in participation has to do as much as anything else with a near-boundless mistrust for anything that smells like a political organization. That's why, when Murúa ran for deputy for the Province of Buenos Aires on the Frente Polo Social ticket and Diego Kravetz (the MNER's lawyer) for the legislature of the Federal Capital for the PRD, a lot of people reacted by thinking, "this is just more of the same after all." However, others disagreed. Cándido, from the Chilavert Cooperative, felt that:

They're spaces we need to occupy, because otherwise, somebody else will, and they'll do who-knows-what. Because we've already created thousands of jobs without occupying political posts. Imagine what we could do from the inside. We wouldn't play dirty politics. We've already proved we can make factories produce.

Murúa recognizes the risks:

I think there's widespread rejection among our people of the trap in elections. The entire Argentine political class is guilty of fraud. But there's also a demand from the social organizations to sit down and participate at the table with the politicians. We think it's an institutional space that can let the organizations express their politics. It's true that there are a lot of workers who felt disappointed by my political advance. All I know is, of the *compañeros* from the movement that we were able to talk to – mostly in the province of Buenos Aires and the capital city – there wasn't one person who told us not to go for it. Just the opposite. In the cooperative I represent, IMPA, before accepting my candidacy, I asked the *compañeros*, and everybody agreed. It's the possibility of having one more Deputy. Even I'm not convinced you can get much done there. What I'm going to do – at least this is what I try to do today, and my *compañeros* will verify if I do it or not – is be in every fight, like I have up until now. This could be a step towards building something bigger.

One of the practical problems in this decision is the lack of structures within the MNER. Who's going to take your place in all the conflicts?

This is almost a philosophical question, whether cadres are born or made. I think it's a little of both. We try to form cadres, and I don't know if we do a very good job. Maybe we should make demands on the *compañeros* like they make demands on us. You don't have to be some big lawyer to recover a factory. You have to have a political decision by the workers, and two or three *compañeros* to guide the process. When we move on, other *compañeros* will appear who aren't so visible now. Same goes for me – my work won't be in Congress, but in each conflict, like always. What I won't be able to do, and I talked to my *compañeros* at IMPA about this, is run the business. The movement is fed by other figures with combative pasts and surprising dedication, who stand up with the workers in the fight and eventually join one of the cooperatives.

Interview with Eduardo Murúa and Diego Kravetz

After a lot of informal encounters, at the beginning of May, we interviewed Diego Kravetz and Eduardo Murúa at length in the BAUEN Hotel. The chat, with one of the leaders of the MNER and one of the lawyers who knows most about the legal ins and outs of the recovered factories, was riddled with jokes, especially once the camera was turned off. In a way, these two men want to live up to what they believe is expected of them. Each phrase Murúa uses is chosen, and the tone of conviction he uses is not casual. "If others follow us, great, but either way, we'll keep fighting," his tone seems to say. This stubbornness allows them to keep going without worrying too much about the endless obstacles to be sorted out. At the beginning of the interview neither of their cell phones would stop ringing until, after five minutes, they finally just turned them off. Even then, someone who knew where Kravetz was called to let him know they urgently needed him.

During this chat, led by Avi, we were able to talk at length about the real objectives of the movement, its limitations, and the possibility that they might actually be keeping the lid on a social situation at the boiling point.

Avi: Explain to us the basic ideas of the movement of recovered businesses.

Eduardo Murúa: At its core, the movement is a new way to struggle that Argentine workers have got because of a concrete fact – the massive unemployment across the country. Since '96 or '97, the country has been suffering unemployment of 30%. The usual union struggle didn't reach us, because the businesses went bankrupt, and we workers were left structurally unemployed. So, what we all imagined was a better way to struggle, which was to have the means of production and make them produce through self-management. That's what's central: the continuity of collective struggle, which is a very important historical experience for the Argentine workers' movement, because this kind of situation has been going on since '69, but only now has this new method of struggle been chosen. That's what we are today, a reflection of that experience, and of the workers' political decision to give the labor struggle a new dynamic, to continue the struggle by taking over factories and making them produce, forced by the circumstances of unemployment we're living through in our country.

A: Is there a strategy to make this all as contagious as we've seen?

EM: No, we don't have a strategy or anything like that. We do what we can. What you saw is a movement of poor people. We really don't have a big structure. It's just the workers and the workers' decisions. Sometimes it can be hard for us to be everywhere. I think if the movement was better organized, better structured, and had some kind of economic structure, we could go much further, and occupy more factories. People want to fight, they want their jobs back, but we still don't have the tools to become exponentially stronger.

A: We've seen a lot of different ways to struggle throughout the world that abandon traditional paths. There's a new impatience in people that are looking for their own solutions without waiting for the government to give them what they need. Do you feel connected to these people in some way?

EM: Yes – I think we're all suffering the attack of neoliberalism and globalization, and I think the coming struggles will have to do with this. The level of unemployment in the world is profound, and it has no solution without a change in the system, with different institutions that distribute the wealth in a different way. So, these types of struggle will continue, because the technological revolution going on in the world makes you think about a new society – not one based on work, but on another kind of distribution, another kind of organization. That's why this kind of struggle is going on in the world, and why we're doing it here. Maybe we're not that connected, but certainly we have the same strength and the same expectations of changing this economic system that's oppressing most of the world's population.

Diego Kravetz: Like Eduardo said. I don't think there's anything in the world of laws today that can contain the real-life situation people are living in. I mean, people's problem with the world of laws is that the institutions, the way they are now, can't provide solutions to the needs they're living with because of the economic system. That's where the discord comes from: there are takeovers here, takeovers there, problems when it comes to action. Simply because the world of laws has no tools to meet the basic needs of the population of Argentina and other parts of the world.

A: You're the one who goes to the court and tells the judge the workers have the right to take over a factory they didn't buy. What are the legal arguments you use so they'll allow this?

DK: At some point, the law understood the needs of the people. Some rights never went into effect, but they did manage to get them in some places. For example, the right to work, or to have a house, are rights that are not only constitutional, but also at a higher level, partly because there are international treaties that Argentina is part of, that talk about these. What you do is look for legal rights in some law, some rule, even in nature itself, and try to breathe some life into that right that was left there for dead back in the history of Argentina, or of the world. Put into practice today, that means that the workers have a concrete and functional right to work, which is more important morally and politically than the right to property. And then, from there, you look for the legal shortcuts, knowing full well that – I mean, let's not kid ourselves. With talk that's just political and moral, obviously, you're not going to get anywhere, and with a constitutional right that might as well be dead, you're not going to get anywhere, either. So, it's very important to also know the rules of the system. Above all, a lot about commercial law, because the trap is in their own laws, so you look for the loophole to recover the jobs.

A: In North America, we've been programmed to believe that private property is the basis of society, and all the rest is built on that. How would you respond to that?

DK: I think it's a fallacy they've created for themselves. It's a mindset. Not even in the laws of the U.S. is the right to property absolute. They even have a bankruptcy law that's much better than ours, which clearly demonstrates this. Their famous Chapter 11, for example, lets them put the jobs of thousands of workers in the aeronautical industry over the right to property. If the right to private property were absolute, the creditors would be first, and everything would be liquidated to cover those who put up money for the aeronautics industry. But they decided that well-being is a higher value, the well-being of their people, and the right of thousands of aeronautical employees to work. This case is a great example. The right to private property makes for good talk, like talk from the North often is, but internally, the talk is asymmetrical, because there, it's treated differently. Inside, they're allowed mechanisms to get past situations that they won't let us get past. Even though on the outside, they say the right to property is most important, on the inside, they demonstrate every day that they're worried about keeping the system going for the good of important social sectors, pushing the right to property off to the side a bit.

A: What do you think of Kirchner?

EM: I think he's going to have an historic opportunity to at least be Argentina's Cardoso, and be a sort of hinge between the old and the new that our country could have. A different political force could be consolidated – maybe not exactly a socialist revolution, but still a serious change in the country with respect to the world. We weren't militants or anything close, bah, we were militants, but in the '70s. Kirchner belonged to the *Peronista* Youth in those days. But we don't have very high expectations for Kirchner, not the way we do for our people's politics, our people's fight, our society's fight. Certainly, on May 26th we'll be opponents. He may not do what our people need, what our country needs, but I do think a possibility has opened up to build something new, and in the next elections to start proposing something new.

A: Another basic question: How many occupied factories are there in our country, and how many workers are in them?

EM: Today there are 162 recovered factories, almost 13,000 jobs. But there are still no studies on it. Like I was telling you before, this is a new way for workers to struggle. I'm sure in a lot of other places in the country where we can't reach, there are workers recovering their factory. But those are the figures, more or less.

A: Could you tell me what the situation is like right now? Is it growing, taking off, does it have strength?

EM: There's exponential growth, very strong growth of this experience and of these new ways to struggle, and there's a very strong commitment on the part of society toward these workers, and this movement has a talk that no other talk can stand up to. Not even the most reactionary sectors in society question the idea of workers recovering their jobs, recovering their businesses. We believe that in a short time, with the mobilization and with the demonstration of what the workers can do, not only will we have these jobs, but many more, because we're going to get policies from the State. I think we're going to force the State to make a policy on this sector. We always say that if there were State policies for this sector of the population, if there was a modification of of the bankruptcy law, in a short time, a million jobs could be recovered.

A: What do you want to change within the bankruptcy law?

EM: Basically, for each business that goes bankrupt to be put in the workers' hands. That no businesses be liquidated. For us, businesses are social goods, not private goods. Those businesses were built by their workers, not just by the capital the boss provided. And in Argentina, very little capital is provided – it all depends on the workers' efforts. On the other hand, we also want the national government to create a fiduciary fund for start-up capital. That would give a lot of power to the recovered businesses, which would let them bring a lot more workers on board. In many of the businesses we've recovered, there are a fifth of the workers there used to be. That's what we want to build, businesses with as many workers as possible, like we did in IMPA: there were 40 of us workers that started, and today, there are 174 of us.

A: We talked with the Brukman brothers' lawyer, and he explained to me that there's no respect for the right to private property in Argentina, that the recovered factories might be good for some workers in some places, but if you change the bankruptcy law so that every factory ends up in the hands of the workers... How do you explain to society as a whole that this can be good for everyone?

EM: We haven't stayed with any business that hasn't had labor trouble, hasn't been abandoned, or has paid the workers' salaries and benefits. We're not saying we never will – we're not promising anything.

But so far, it's been a struggle for the dignity of the workers and to keep being an active part of production in this country. The dispute is not with the factories that are working, but in the factories that are empty today, the ones the bosses abandoned, or the factories that are already bankrupt and that the bosses can't say anything about, because they aren't theirs any more.

A: But you want the struggle to grow and occupy factories that are open, not just the ones that are sitting empty.

EM: I wouldn't propose this for all factories. We know the general structure of our country and our diagnosis that we have is that there's external aggression, a commercial war of central power against our country, against our region, to keep us from developing. Within this framework and this diagnosis that we have, we defend our jobs, our homeland. We do have a definite confrontation at the macroeconomic level with the big monopolies, but generally not with small and medium businesses. I think we suffer the same aggression by international monopolies and national monopolies. There, I do think there needs to be a major intervention on the part of the State together with the workers to put a stop these sectors' aggression against national industry. Today, I represent *compañeros* who want to recover their jobs, and we also support workers busy in capitalist businesses who are struggling for their salaries and for better working conditions. I also think it's a fight to reduce work hours in capitalist businesses. But, I would say that, at least today, I don't propose putting every business in the hands of the workers.

A: The day after the elections, the IMF came to the city to start talks with both possible Presidents of Argentina [the winners of the first round, Carlos Menem and Néstor Kirchner –EM] to explain their concern about the threat to private property in Argentina. What type of threat does the movement represent to the IMF because of its ideas?

E: The IMF is the central power in Argentina representing the policies of the central countries, of imperialism. I think they want to impose, or maintain, a model of social exclusion, a model without industries, which means that everything the IMF is proposing is going to affect the recovered businesses to some degree. Anyway, everything we've done outside the law –even though it's legitimate – we're going to keep doing, independent of the IMF and the presidential candidates. This is a concrete need the people have, and it won't stop for laws or dictates from the IMF. And also, I think they represent the enemy of the region, of an underdeveloped country, not because they're evil, but because they also see that their system is falling to pieces, and that it's impossible to keep it going if they don't invade our countries, if they can't stop the development of our region.

A: So, the question is: How do you fight these powers? Because the new government is going to make an agreement with the IMF, and the IMF is going to say, "Fine, but you have to do something about the recovered factories," and boom, the movement's gone.

EM: It would be an honor if the IMF noticed us, if the IMF considered us an important enemy, and assigned the managers of democracy the task of getting rid of the recovered businesses. I don't think we'll have that honor, but just like they tried to impose other things on us – a military coup, disappearances of our *compañeros*, death, jail – it'll be up to the next government to decide if it wants to repeat all that, if, instead of in a factory we'll be in jail, or we'll be disappeared, or somehow faced with this power that only answers to another central power.

A: You challenged the IMF in court. Tell me how that went, and why you did it.

DK: The topic of the de-industrialization of Argentina operates, at least broadly speaking, on three sets of rules. The first set is customs rules. The second was the credit rules of the Central Bank, which were as bad for cooperatives as they were for small and medium businesses in general. A big part of the avalanche of bankruptcies was caused by the credit rules of the Central Bank. And the third set of rules was the law that Cavallo modified, which is the bankruptcy law. We fight hard against the IMF because of what it ended up doing with the bankruptcy law. After the people toppled De la Rúa, just a few days later, the legislators decided to make a couple of modifications to the bankruptcy law because they knew very well that there was no real possibility of fulfilling contracts, and obviously, there was no possibility of fulfilling an agreement during a dispute. So, the flood of bankruptcies would have been bigger, even worse than it was. Then they decided to have a series of suspensions of the bankruptcy law that they ended up voting for unanimously.

When we fought with the IMF, we did it in defense of the suspensions that avoided more bankruptcies. Around May of 2002, the IMF put a lot of pressure on the executive and legislative branches both to roll back the suspension of the bankruptcy law and to get the law of economic subversion passed. The way they did it, and the huge pressure they used, amounted to extortion, as far as we were concerned, and that's a crime. What we were asking for, to be exact, was for the director of the IMF and [U.S.] Treasury Secretary Paul O'Neill to be jailed, they were constantly threatening that if the country didn't back down, it was going to go badly for us. So we decided to come out in defense of Argentine institutions and of every one of the legislators. At IMPA, which is a disputed business, we came out against the situation, which was a clear threat to us that was all over the media. When O'Neill came to Argentina, we asked for an arrest warrant. We tried to have him thrown in jail, so he couldn't escape trial. Well, the trial was called off. What I see as important in this experience is we never hid, and that's what the legislators should have done, and we told them so. I guess I see it as one more commitment in the struggle. Even though it wasn't in the streets, I think it was still part of the struggle against central power.

A: One of the things I'm interested to learn about is your idea on how the massive unemployment in this country is politicizing the people, actually creating the conditions for people to start taking control of their lives this way.

EM: The history of the Left in this country has always been very limited, and many times, it's committed very important betrayals that the Argentine people still remember. If there's been a Left here, a formal Left, it's always been part of *Peronismo*. That's probably why you don't see see much of the Left, but you will see *compañeros* who come out of *Peronismo* with an important history in the labor movement. But in other cases, they don't even have this, they're *compañeros* that recover their businesses. For us, to advance in terms of the conscience of these *compañeros* is very important. Making progress and understanding the situation doesn't just mean their knowing how a factory works, and how well-being can be distributed better, but also their starting to see the whole national problem, and how the country is being managed, and the situation this business is in and why it can't work as a business, the function of the monopolies, the function of the legal and financial systems in stopping all these developments. I think this is the most important part of the movement. And I think this forms the political vision of the *compañeros* that are now part of the occupied factories, who are interested in the whole national reality. Their experience in the struggle has raised their consciousness quickly.

A: You have a unique perspective on how this process changes people, because between you two, you've probably seen more of the struggle in Argentina that anyone else. Could you give me some examples, as specifically as possible, of how relationships between people change in this struggle to recover work?

D: I've seen big and small things. One little thing was, I saw a *compañero* who had never been in a street fight with the police stand at the front of the group and tell everyone not to give the documents to the police, and tell the police they can't have the documents. The growth in this type of *compañero*, who had never been in this kind of struggle and who steps up to the front, or climbs on top of a tank, with a bottle full of gas to defend his factory. And how they start to see the relationship between their struggle and those of the other factories. I think one of the most important things for workers when they recover their factory is their dignity. I think they're dying to – you might say they're killing themselves – to be able to transform themselves into new people. Not to idealize or romanticize this group of workers, but I'm talking about any of these *compañeros* who did just that. They say you're free when you kill what's oppressing you, and I think this process makes a *compañero* fight and throw off any part of himself that was resigned, that was passive, that could accept anything, and give way to this new person. I think that's what you see most. Changing your mind, your head, the way you think, is the hardest thing of all. I've seen workers who were waiting for their bosses to come back suddenly commit to defend what's theirs, even if that meant going to jail, and these are very big changes for the workers.

My role as a lawyer is different from the struggle in the streets. I mean, I've gone, and I've been hit a time or two, but I'm not the one suffering police repression. You have to keep that in mind when you talk to the *compañeros* from the place I talk to them from, which is a place where I'm unlikely to have to pay the consequences of the struggle. And the truth is, you talk, and they get it, and they go beyond anything you'd ever believe. And what you see... It's very exciting to see the way they defend themselves, and how far they'll go. I mean, they've lost everything, they have no salary, they have no boss, they have no house, they have nothing. They transform, and when the police come and beat the shit out of them, instead of protecting themselves (any more than anyone else would, of course), they face very violent situations together. I think it's incredible, very impressive. And this is all because they changed the way they think. That's what happened, for example, at Crometálica the first day, the first month, when some even went to jail – they fought, and they withstood it. That case is a great example. I've seen people transform when a *compañero* gets hit. I've seen *compañeros* in IMPA that are very calm, in violent situations, including the older ones, who jump up and fight with the police. Police in helmets.

A: Why is this movement taking place in Argentina and not somewhere else?

EM: You're going say it's my pride talking, but the truth is, I think it has to do with the experience of the labor movement. Of all Latin America, Argentine workers are the best. The structure of the Argentine unions and the struggles carried out by this movement were very important. And, I think it basically has to do with the experience of a country that's never had unemployment of more than 4 or 5%, and the fact that we're ready to live by our work. I think these are the two basic conditions: a labor movement whose history is deeply rooted in our consciences, and a country that considers work a defining element of a person.

A: Maybe I'm wrong, but could it be that the famous Argentine middle class has created the idea that everyone has a right to more?

EM: I think so, it also has to do with that. That's what I was saying before about society as a whole. And that's how it is for this movement of recovered factories. If it hadn't been for the people's support of our struggle, the legal system and the police would have come down harder on us, and they would have thrown us out of many more factories. Yeah, I think the Argentine middle class has a lot to do with this, and has a lot to do with the working class.

A: Let's talk a little about democracy. Honestly, do you think people are ready for democracy in their workplace?

EM: Yes, we're absolutely convinced of that. That's what we want, and we're going to try to keep that way forever. Of course, not everyone is prepared to make decisions in an occupied factory, but I think in a country like ours, which is occupied, we should have that kind of democracy – not a representative democracy, but a more direct democracy. There would have to be more referendums and more consultations with the people on important topics. The nation has to decide on strategic matters. You can't say you have a democracy and then not do what the people tell you. Not just in Argentina – in Spain, too. 90% of the people opposed the war, but the feudal lord, the friend of the king, said they had to go to war. So, it's not just in Argentina that we don't have a true democracy, but all over. That's why I say the people are prepared to decide on the most important things, that they won't go wrong. When power is in the hands of the people, the government can't go wrong. That's what happens in the factories in our country, and that's why we want democracy, not just in the factories, but in the whole country.

A: I want to go back to the topic of what's possible. Are we sure we're not just going as far as they're letting us?

EM: No. At least, I'm not sure. But I know they don't want this. I don't know if the system is going to be able to use us, if that's what you're asking. What I do know is that we want each occupied factory to be a trench for the final battle. We know we're just one small corner of the great struggle of our people. We want our businesses to become a space to struggle for our country. I don't think we can achieve national liberation by ourselves. I don't think we're that important, but we believe many of the spaces that have been recovered are going to be the trenches, and are going to help.

And I don't think we have anything to do with them, because so far, they haven't given us anything. We're not even working, as far as their policies are concerned. None of us has any commitment to the dominant sectors of the country. They think maybe we can recover a business here or there, but that we're not going to be able to affect the system as a whole. And that may be true, for now. If this doesn't turn into what we want – trenches of the final battle – it'll be one more experience of social struggle, but our intention is to make it something more. The important thing is the change produced in each *compañero* in each recovered factory. This is what we have to work for. We try to make a little progress on this every day. If we don't have the right people in the right places to understand this reality, to go from being a worker to someone political and revolutionary, capable of working with the rest of the people for national liberation... but that's a task for another day. At least we know that's what we want, although I don't know if we're going to achieve it everywhere.

3. THE PILLARS OF THE RECOVERED BUSINESSES

In this section, we'll look at some of the key points in the phenomenon of recovered businesses. The strongest examples were chosen to explain them in social, economic and legal terms. The changes in these spheres are bringing about the political transformation that weaves through the following analysis.

3.1. The recovered society

> *The phantoms formed in the human brain are also, necessarily, sublimates of their material life-process, which is empirically verifiable and bound to material premises.*[46]

The German Ideology, *Karl Marx*, 1968

One of the motivations for this analysis of recovered businesses is to examine their ability to change their participants and, therefore, society. Of course, their real development depends on a lot of factors, but when you look into it, you see they have strengths that are a cause for optimism, especially the changes that take place in the workers struggling and organizing with their peers.

The impact of recovered factories goes far beyond their actual dimensions. Their real power lies in the fact that they change the nature of work. Work is one of the biggest parts of life, both quantitatively, because of all the hours it takes up, and qualitatively, because of its essential role in sustaining life for the worker and his or her family. Even for people who don't work in a recovered business, the mere existence of such a development

---

[46] Translator's note: Translation taken from http://www.usp.nus.edu.sg/post/poldiscourse/marxideology.html.

allows them to imagine other solutions to any crisis that might happen at their workplace. As employees, they're subject to a boss who can withdraw his capital and send them home jobless.

To understand this better, a number of researchers are evaluating the influence the recovered factories have had on a large part of the working class.

> ...in spite of how recent this phenomenon is, and also the difficulty in establishing its impact through the building of a new worker identity, recovering factories doubtlessly represents a cultural watershed. It offers the possibility of identifying elements linked to processes of collective construction.[47]

How is this new way of organizing work being lived out? It's hard to explain. In mid-19th century Cuba, reading circles began to appear in prisons, in which groups of prisoners making cigars were able to listen as they worked. This custom was taken up by workers in cigar factories, many of whom were anarchists. They took advantage of the quiet nature of the task in order to read aloud from texts that were more and more political. There's a bit of this "poetic" atmosphere in the recovered factories. The right to drink *mate* (always with a lot of sugar, as I discovered to my surprise) is one of the most important daily successes. When the noise level allows it, conversation is cordial and generally relaxed – a great improvement over the way in which life on the factory floor was previously organized. The workers are proud of this change, and when they happen to be doing something that was formerly forbidden, they talk tirelessly about the injustices they used to experience.

3.1.1. Daily life and ideology

> *We now believe that the working class, given its daily experience, has the capacity to share the management of the economy with business, and we can even assure you that business will be more efficient, which is not to say that businesses are not efficient enough. There is also no doubt that the participation of the working class actually [...] would have avoided many problems.*
>
> *Augustín Tosco, from Augustín Tosco: Present in the struggles of the working class.*

In one of the most interesting sections of his work – in that it leads to a profound understanding of the complexity and difficulty of social change – Karl Marx explains the basis of historical materialism. According to him, material life and the daily practices in which an individual lives

---

[47] Palomino, H. et al., 1/2003.

and works determine ideology, not the reverse. You don't need to become an orthodox structuralist to see that this is a powerful tool for understanding change. There's no need to dwell on this, because there are countless books and studies that analyze it in detail. Instead, let's look at a brief part that will be useful in understanding the recovered factories and why they have such enormous potential for deeper change. In *The German Ideology*, Marx explains:

> Real life is not determined by consciousness, but rather consciousness by real life. In the first case, the starting point is consciousness considered as the living person. In the second case, which is real life, the starting point is real, living individuals, and consciousness is considered only as their consciousness.[48]

To put it more simply, it's everyday life, the concrete actions at work, the food we eat, the way our family life is organized, how we prepare our meals, our sleep patterns – the day-to-day routines – that frame our thinking. If we spend our days tightening bolts, like Charlie Chaplin in *Modern Times*, we probably have little time for reading, and we may see our lives as a series of mechanical, repetitive actions. We probably have explanations for the routine nature of our lives and find it normal that others make all the decisions. All this reinforces our daily behavior. So, in every concrete act of life there's an implicit view or ideology, which has arisen and is the result of those same acts. This interpretation of the concept of praxis described by Marx is shared by many authors:

> Marx's decisive intuition is, simply, that the way men [sic] understand and interpret their lives is not free, but depends on it and is rooted in it. This is why he famously said that "it is not men's consciousness that determines their lives, it is their lives that determines their consciousness." It is life, one's own personal, individual life, the concrete, daily activities, and not a pre-existing, objective ideology.[49]

To some degree, these daily activities – praxis[50] – in our societies tend to be based on pyramidal structures of hierarchy and top-down power. Naturally, this mechanism also occurs in factories, where workers are not free to use their own criteria beyond what's required of them. For example, in a factory the arrangement of the machines determines who communicates with who. Where the bosses place themselves determines the level of control they have over the workers and the ability of the workers to organize in the face of a decision with which they disagree. Whether or not there are common spaces and whether workers eat together or at their

---

[48] Marx, Karl. 1968, pg. 12.
[49] Michel, Henry, 1984.
[50] For a better understanding of the concept of praxis, see Henry Michel, 1984.

machines (as was the case in Brukman) are factors in how well workers get to know each other and form bonds.

Raúl Godoy, a worker at Zanón, said that at the factory, workers' uniforms were different colors for different tasks. This let the managers determine at a glance who was out of their work area. He also described the colored lines on the floor indicating permitted paths through the factory. There were also supervision windows at various points. Clearly, there was an intent to control the people at the factory, which limited their ability to build friendships or exchange opinions. Many people found these measures unjust, or at least excessive, in the light of their pre-work experiences, such as family structure, education, friendships, and so on. In the best of cases, they rebelled against these measures, but many others accepted them as just one more experience where domination and authority naturally emanate from someone else.

It follows that a change in the way a workplace is organized has a series of implications for the way workers approach life itself. A worker-controlled factory sees things from a different perspective. There is no one else to blame, because decisions are made together. There's no boss telling each of the workers what to do. You have to think while you work. Each person has a voice and a vote. There's no boss to blame for what's done or not done. Understanding this profound change is essential to grasping the impact that owning the means of production has on people.

Those workers who were able to struggle against feelings of resignation and who dared to recover their job were able to do so only when confronted, *en masse*, by the material limits of survival. In a country where another job could be found, most of these workers probably would have moved on to look for it, even knowing they would once again face injustice, exploitation and control. In many cases, resignation would be the normal reaction to losing a job, but large-scale unemployment means deprivation. With their backs to the wall, the workers were forced to transform resignation into a personal energy many didn't even know they had. In a study done in the recovered factory Grissinópoli, the author explains that the workers "discovered new powers within themselves – both collectively and individually."[51]

Although the workers may believe in ideals of justice and equality based on their schooling or their family experience, they may well find themselves unable to practice them in a system built on punishment and often direct humiliation.[52] In contrast, a new way of organizing work based

[51] Hazaki, César, "Crónica de una lucha obrera," in Carpintero, Enrique and Hernández, Mario, 2002.

[52] Examples of these daily humiliations, and not just the obvious non-payment of wages and the theft of countless paycheck deductions, are a common topic of discussion in recovered factories. Only a few are recounted in this book, but I hope they are sufficient to give the reader an idea of the situations a worker faces in a system with a very unequal balance of power.

on a sense of unity among the workers forces them to develop these facets of their personalities – including workers who never had them, and those in whom they'd been dormant for many obedient years. The results of the collision between these new character traits and the old ones left over from a lifetime of hierarchical structures and competition varies from one person to the next. It's safe to say, however, that nobody remains unaffected.

This change was a visible part of many of the transitions we witnessed throughout the study, and when we talked to other people close to what was happening, they agreed. Basically, this is how the transitions would go: at first, the workers only wanted their back pay, and that's all they (timidly) asked of the boss. When the boss gave no answer, or fled, the workers occupied the factory to wait for the answer to their demand. Then there came a time when they refused to accept the crumbs they were offered – or not offered, in many cases. Instead, they decided to fight for a deeper change. Sometimes, this change only came from the certainty that there would be no answer of any kind. These two stages are usually reached when the workers control the factory building. During this time, the workers talk among themselves, gain access to information in the offices, receive clients and suppliers, learn how much of their work went unpaid, etc., and begin to discover the lies to which they'd been subjected.

For example (one of many), the workers of Nueva Esperanza applied for unemployment benefits when they lost their jobs. They found out they were ineligible, because the contributions that had been meticulously deducted from their salaries were never paid into the unemployment fund. Then there was the additional disappointment of the complicity of the unions (with a few exceptions, such as the Metallurgical Union of Quilmes, the Commercial Union of Rosario and the Graphic Workers in the capital). Sometimes the workers are able to channel their anger by working with other groups to build the idea that they can recover their jobs.

In some cases, the situation is resolved before it reaches this point. This happened at Gattik in early 2003, when, faced with the threat of worker occupation, the owners caught up on all the back pay they owed. When issues are not resolved in time, the idea of running the factory (inspired by successful examples) becomes a greater and greater temptation. Many workers begin to flirt with fantasies of owning the factory and enjoying the accompanying privileges, but this is an idea that quickly evaporates: there is no boss, but rather a collective.

We watched the former BAUEN Hotel workers go through this process as they formed the Callao Cooperative. At the first meeting, held in the Chilavert Cooperative's recovered print shop in February 2003, the workers started with a cathartic session. They listed the many injustices they had suffered at the hands of the owners, culminating in the story of how they had been left to run the hotel almost on their own for some time before it closed. Their explanation of how they had already proven they could run the business gradually gave way to a pregnant silence, as it dawned on them that there was a legal framework to do just this, in turn allowing them the possibility to truly keep the fruits of their labor. At that point, the focus of the discussion shifted from negotiating for their back pay to the legal framework they would use for worker control and questions of recovery. Towards the end of the meeting, one of the workers asked what would happen if they used the possibility of worker control as a way to pressure the owners. The brand-new president of the nascent Callao Cooperative replied, "What for? So we can be back in this same situation again in a few months?" When the workers have no alternatives, and begin to imagine themselves as their own bosses, it's very difficult to turn back. A worker at Nueva Esperanza (formerly Grissinópoli) explained it this way:

> This experience has changed our mentality. That means we aren't going to lend ourselves out, or give ourselves away, or sell ourselves out. Now we know we provide a service as workers, and we should be paid for it. That's because our work is part of the dignity and respect that we owe ourselves. Now we know the value of our work, and it must be compensated at its true value. [...] No more little vouchers for AR$20 or for 70. Those were very dark times for us. We're upwards of forty years old. We can't go back to that. We don't have time for that.[53]

At the beginning of the conflict, the workers of Nueva Esperanza wanted a weekly voucher of AR$100. That's a far cry from their present objective of worker control, and farther still from the AR$10 in coins (many of them counterfeit) they were getting at the end of their time with the bosses!

Another anecdotal example is that of the president of a cooperative, an engineer who now has his own small business. Together with Naomi and Avi, we interviewed him for the first time in January of 2003, when he had just begun his battle to recovery a factory. After a long chat in which he told us in detail how he intended to proceed, we asked who he would vote for in the upcoming elections (the date of which was unknown at the time). He replied that he intended to vote for Adolfo Rodríguez Saá for President and Aldo Rico for Governor of the Province of Buenos Aires. I was so perplexed that I had to ask why. "We need a strong hand!" he answered. Seven months later, this man had become one of the most omnipresent activists in the movement for re-claiming factories, and was at almost every meeting we went to, giving a hand to anybody who needed

---

[53] Hazaki, César, "Chronicles of a Workers' Struggle," from Carpintero, Enrique and Hernández, Mario, 2002.

it. At a meeting in early August, he criticized Luis Caro for standing as candidate for mayor of Avellaneda, "and, to top it off, he's on the ballot with Rico and Rodríguez Saá!"

A year after starting their recovery process and a month after the expropriation, the leader of the MNER involved in the FORJA San Martín case told me that

> Recently, some of the workers have started saying, "This is a lot bigger than I ever thought. If we can get this far, we can do anything," and "Now that we've got the cards in our hands, let's see what we can do!" People from other factories come knocking on our door, asking what we've done. They see we've had a big impact around here.

Others studies confirm the impact on the thinking of workers in the struggle:

> As soon as the workers take over a factory, their attention turns from demanding back salaries to questioning the legitimacy of the ownership of productive assets, which are still legally in the hands of the owners or those responsible for bankruptcy proceedings.[54]

The process of taking over a factory can, by itself, change the way reality is perceived:

> The subjective impact and the rupture inherent in the experience of worker control at Brukman gave them a whole new sense of struggle. Even if they did not come from a family with a leftist tradition, it took away their fears and made them appreciate the support they were receiving. Taking over a factory made them question their whole cosmology.[55]

This experience is reflected vividly in one of the reports we did in the documentary on the Chilavert print shop. We talked to Cándido and his son Hernán, who, in spite of his youth, is now a veteran of the struggle to recover the workplace. Avi asked them how the relations between workers had changed since the cooperative started up:

> Cándido: We have the advantage of having known each other for many years. We all had the same clear objectives, and that lets you avoid a lot of trouble. We were all focused on getting the business going, and so you close ranks and work as a team. You can have disagreements about the work, but we're working toward the objective we set out at the beginning, and that makes things easy. When you have a good work atmosphere and no one's getting upset, there might be trouble in production, but if you're relaxed, you deal with it differently. You become like

---

[54] Palomino, H. et al., 1/2003.
[55] Chavez, María, et al., "Brukman Under Worker Control."

a family. For example, we eat together, we try to share activities in the street, because it's not just about the work in the plant – it's also about what we do outside. The truth is, we're having a good time.

Avi: I've always been curious about how hard it is to change the relationships among the workers. Let's suppose you've been working alongside the same guy for twenty years. And one of the things you've been doing together for the past twenty years is bitching about the boss. Everyone complains about the boss. Those two (points to the sound technician[56] and cameraman) complain about me –everybody does that. I gripe about my bosses in Toronto. Sometimes what brings the workers together is that they are all suffering under the same system. But what happens when a problem comes up and it's just as much your fault as it is the fault of the guy next to you?

Hernán: That's tough, it's true. There's one person who takes the initiative to take over the factory, and in my experience, that's the one who takes initiative on the job. Right? But I think this is a question of consciousness, of commitment. You can commit to making the factory work efficiently and produce what it's supposed to produce, but you might also decide that you want to do more and say, "No, I'm not going to leave it at that. I'm going further." That's not to diminish the role of the other guy who does what he should, but we're the ones who go the extra mile, like it says in the Bible: "If anyone asks you to carry their burden one mile, carry it two." I think that's the commitment these two [he nods in the direction of his father and Ernesto] have taken on.

Cándido: We all made the commitment. You realize that when you see a piece of finished work. If we, as workers, felt pride when we produced a good piece of work before, just imagine how we feel now that we are the creators of this work – we're all the prouder. We feel good, and the underlying principle is responsibility. We've been talking about responsibility from the very beginning. We really emphasize that. There are no bosses here, only responsibilities. The guy who used to sweep and clean up had fewer responsibilities before. Now he has the same responsibilities as anyone else. So as you can see, responsibility is a big thing with us. The work has to turn out well, it has to be top quality and we are all responsible for it, not just one or two of us. We don't delegate responsibility to one or two individuals. Sharing the responsibility is giving us good results.

Hernán: As each person's responsibility increases, the efficiency of our business increases. It's mathematical. Each worker wants to assure that the next document that's printed, or cut that's made, is the best yet, and that makes for greater efficiency. You begin to realize that all this is yours. I think that's the hardest part. We were talking about that with someone from the BAUEN. You know, maybe this print shop is like our own home. When I was eight years old, I would bring my dad his supper if he had to work late. Over at the BAUEN, it's a different story... a hotel that's worth 14 million dollars. You stand at the door and look in and you think, "All this?" So for them, the process of making it all happen is a bit different. Some people like this more, and make things happen faster, but I think it's the same process as at Chilavert. And nobody is the same as they were the first day. As time passes, our commitment to our own business and also to others' work grows. You'd think it would be the other way around: as soon as we had our

---

[56] *Translator's note: The sound technician was Esteban Magnani.*

own problems solved, the hell with everyone else. But no, it's just the opposite. Our commitment to other businesses got stronger, and we were always on the phone to other business, asking how things were going. And then they would call back and tell us their news, and we would pass it on and everybody would be happy to hear the good news if they won their case. This sense of commitment and responsibility grew with time, as our consciousness awakened. It takes a bit longer for some than for others, but everyone has decided to stand on one side of the fence and not on the other. Nobody can guess what will happen next, but I think there will be growth.

As I said above, this change in daily practices is, to varying degrees, transforming people's reality. They come from many schools of thought but can't help but be changed all the same. You see another element in this model of transformation when you ask what happens when more workers are needed. The initial answer, generally, is to take on new people for lower pay, that is, to reproduce the same hierarchical system they'd lived in before. However, as far as I can tell from my research, this has not actually happened in any of the recovered businesses (the system in place at Unión y Fuerza, as we'll see, has some special provisions for new members, but this doesn't contradict the argument). Cooperatives generally take in new people on a trial basis for three or six months, and after that, the assembly votes on incorporating the person into the cooperative with the same rights as everyone else. This is how new workers are incorporated into IMPA, the Institute of Communications, Chilavert, Zanón, and others.

In the story of the general coordinator of Zanón, Carlos Saavedra, better known as Manotas (Big Hands), we see another example of the metamorphosis that can happen in a person when the organization of his workplace changes

> Well, before we just took orders. There were 82 supervisors. I have to admit, I was one of them. I joined the struggle, but I was one of them. Only two of us are left from the 82 supervisors. There was a lot of pressure about time and absenteeism. The company wasn't interested in hearing about the workers' personal problems. There was a strict schedule for the tea break. *Mate* was forbidden, and all we did all day long was take orders. Now that's all changed. We don't take orders any more. Each worker runs their machine knowing that what he or she is doing is for all of us. No one has to give us orders. We can drink *mate* whenever we want to, and what 82 people used to do, all 300 of us do nowadays. But we do it conscientiously. We don't need a boss to tell us what to do or how to do it. But we do tell our *compañeros* what we are going to do. We're all taking this risk; it's not just a few people who are committed. Before, when there were bosses, we supervisors had to look in the garbage to see if anyone had been drinking *mate*. That was ridiculous. Now, I want my co-workers to drink *mate*!

With the disappearance of the boss, the whole pattern of work changes. Workers can no longer wait for orders, knowing that at least there will be a paycheck at the end of the month. While this is a sign of success, it's such a deep change that stress is a daily feature of workers' lives. Divorces and separations are fairly common among those swept up in the struggle. A study at Brukman showed that:

> ...the factory goes beyond being a workspace, and becomes a living space. Some workers spend most of the week there to avoid transportation costs; others live there because they are homeless, or because of family conflicts.[57]

In some factories, such as Zanón, they've even set up group therapy to deal with stress. According to a study carried out by another group of researchers on recovered businesses, these new relationships can be summed up this way:

> The "family" relationship that used to exist was very paternalistic. After recovery, it's gradually replaced with a "family" relationship between the workers who took part in the process. These relationships weren't just transformed in the daily working space. The recovery itself made it possible to form strong bonds between and among the workers.[58]

Still, it would be a mistake to think that all the workers at a given factory will inevitably reach the same level of transformation. One of the members of the MNER expressed disappointment at the slow progress he was seeing in the assemblies at a factory where he had been active for almost a year. "When someone who used to be a supervisor speaks, how can you keep everyone from thinking it's gospel? Tell me – how?" More than a few workers have gotten stuck at the halfway point. They resist deep change or a horizontal way of organizing, and cling to selfish ways that have no place in such a factory. A worker in a print shop complained,

> The other day a worker stood up in the assembly and said he wanted a raise. What can you do with a guy like that? He just doesn't get it at all.

The thing is that work, for all the time and intensity a person might put in to it, is not all of life. Many times, it's competing with an awful lot. I was talking with Lalo from MNER about this, and he said,

> At first in FORJA, we voted that the highest salary could not be three times the lowest. We haven't discussed the matter for some time, but I think that there has been a slide towards selfishness. That's sad, but we'll see. There is always the

---

[57] Fernández Alvarez, María Inés, "Transformaciones en el mundo del trabajo y procesos de ocupación/recuperación de fábricas," 12/17 and 18/2002.

[58] Palomino, H, et al., 1/2003.

danger that you'll end up with ten managers who put the rest to work. But still, I also see a trend towards deeper consciousness. Where each *compañero* ends up depends on him or her.

This is a very deep change. The most flexible individuals go along, little by little, scarcely noticing the process. Others may be more resistant to change, and stop halfway through – enough to be part of the new undertaking, but still set in their old ways. Others don't even realize what's happening, or reject the possibility that they could be part of something so foreign to their way of thinking. How far each individual is willing to go is a personal matter and impossible to predict. Just the same, a trail has been blazed, and a new direction charted. After so many years devoid of options, this, in itself, is a revolution – a great, silent change.

3.1.2. The outside world

The transformation of the workplace brings the workers into many conflicts, and not only internal ones. One of the most serious, which appeared throughout the research done for this book, is the difficulty they face making a factory work. Supposedly they lack the responsibility, knowledge, and the drive they need – not to mention the capital. A member of the Lavalán Cooperative, in Ledesma, told an interviewer,

> The bosses wanted to kick us out by force. They told us, "You think you're going to set up a cooperative? You're just a bunch of peons who know nothing about running a factory," but now we're running the factory, and doing it very well. We've produced 250,000 kilos in 20 days without anyone telling us what to do. That's less time than the old boss did it in.[59]

It's easy to understand that if the responsibility for work being done well is left up to the boss, then that's who has to keep after the employees – they don't need to worry about it. This is a headache for researchers studying relations within a given business, looking for an alternative to outright coercion relying on threats of pay cuts or outright dismissals. Such businesses try to push workers' emotional buttons so they'll feel like "part of the family," namely the business. What is good for the business is good for everyone. And they're not wrong. The problem is that labor relations in traditional capitalist business have limits that simply do not allow this kind of identification. In the overwhelming majority of cases, the best they can do is get employees to play the game and do what's expected of them out of self-interest, not because they really feel like they're part of anything. There remains little doubt who is part of the family when it's time for layoffs, or when not all

---

[59] *Abrecaminos*, No. 1, December 2002.

the salaries are paid, or when tough decisions need to be made. At best, the workers are part of someone else's team. They're expendable and can be dismissed, even if it is a painful decision for the bosses.

In a worker-controlled factory, after a lengthy process, responsibility tends to be shared. The workers know that they really are part of the business. This is why, for example, the Yaguané workers came out on June 20th to protest against their unfair exclusion from a meat-export quota for the European Union. This kind of activity seems quite unlikely in a business made up of employees.

Still, it's clear in cooperatives that not everyone has the same level of commitment, and that there are leaders. Not everyone likes to talk a lot, and many continue waiting for solutions from outside, even if "outside" now means inside the assembly. On the other hand, it's also true that more and more workers are getting up the courage to speak their minds simply because the channels are there, open and available for use. Now the limitations are more internal and personal. It's even conceivable that the change in systemic relations within the business could have enough of an effect on workers to produce a ripple effect into other spheres of life. We talked about this with Gladys in the Once neighborhood of Buenos Aires during one of our visits to the "México and Jujuy"[60] tent.

> *Esteban Magnani: What was the atmosphere like at Brukman after the owners left?*
>
> Gladys Figueroa: Before, we didn't know anything about the person who worked beside us all day long. When we were on our own, we learned how to defend ourselves, how to speak, to criticize – how to say out loud what we really thought. We all learned how to do that. Before, I used to listen and keep quiet. Now I listen and then, if I think something is not right, I have to speak up. I can't keep quiet. That was one of our mistakes before. If there had been unity among the *compañeros* before, I think we could have presented our demands all together, instead of waiting for our union rep, who was totally paid off, to go and tell them, "Look, we want such-and-such," and we never knew whether she really did tell them or not, but even if she did, we didn't get anything out of it. I think we should have learned before. I'm not exactly sure what we should have done, but now I think that workers who depend on some boss should always get together and go in a group to talk with their employers and pressure them. One person can't do it alone. If I had to work somewhere else and I saw something that wasn't right, some injustice that the workers were suffering, now I'd get together with some other co-workers to complain to who ever's not doing right – to their face. And if some agreed with me but were afraid of a backlash, we'd have to try to make them see why things happen the way they do in workplaces.

Another important change is going from thinking individually to collectively. Once people start to feel like they are part of something bigger,

---

[60] Editor's note: A street corner in the neighborhood.

something in which they can really participate and make decisions that affect their everyday reality, it's hard to go back. That's what stood out chatting with Gladys, who admitted politics in general didn't really interest her.

EM: Can you imagine yourself working in a normal workplace after being your own boss for a year and a half?

GF: Me, not as a Brukman worker? Well, I'm a skilled worker. I don't know how I would feel. I suppose I'd adapt back, but no boss is going to walk all over me ever again, that's for sure. It would be hard for me to adapt, but they're not going to screw me over again, that's for sure.

These internal loyalties, at times, extend to other businesses as well. One researcher who looked at Nueva Esperanza said that in many of the businesses, they feel that "their destiny is inextricably bound to the bigger picture of the struggles of this social movement."[61] This feeling is intensified by the precariousness of most of the expropriations, where final ownership is not guaranteed. The workers are well aware that when the final fight comes, they'll need the support of their peers. This is reflected in a phrase they often repeat: "What touches one touches us all." Businesses that already have their deed or are about to get it don't necessarily feel as strongly connected to the rest. Roberto Salcedo, the president of the Unión y Fuerza metal foundry, explains that not all the cooperatives necessarily feel like they're part of a wider movement:

That might be the feeling in a brand-new cooperative that's waiting for the expropriation judgment, that has nothing and feels like it depends on the movement and on other cooperatives to put pressure on the government to deal with the expropriation. So, logically, if you belong to a cooperative that is not making any money and you can't make the indemnity payments, then you depend on the wider struggle to convince the government to pay for the expropriation. I don't know what the percentage is, but there must be 20 or 30% that need the movement to get a uniform law passed.

When the processes become stabilized, they can bring about a sort of "bourgeoisification" and an acceptance of the prevailing norms, because these businesses no longer need special laws and are able to compete in the market. The case of Unión y Fuerza is special, because of the way it carried out its struggle with little outside help. It's probably the most stable of the businesses, legally and economically, so it would be hasty to draw general conclusions from this unique case.

There are many more examples that show the change workers go through because of their struggle, and the way they reorganize to start

---

61 Hazaki, César, "Crónica de una lucha obrera," in Carpintero, Enrique and Hernández Mario, 2002.

working. Even though it's still too early to draw general conclusions, and there are cases (like Unión y Fuerza) that could make one think cooperatives might end up locked up like fortresses, there's still a lot reason for hope. To be fair, while Unión y Fuerza workers have disassociated themselves from other cases, they did put their bodies on the line in the Lavalán struggle, and gave money to the Vieytes Cooperative (formerly Ghelco) to start working.

At any rate, it's crucial to understand that any change in the way a worker thinks has to come from inside him or her in a genuine way, if it is to have any real lasting impact. With this in mind, any attempt to force solidarity would be an attack on worker autonomy. This must be avoided at all cost, so their freedom is not co-opted. The road will be long, and certainly not all will make it to the end, but those who do will have played a vital role in blazing a trail toward a deep, desirable social change.

3.1.3. Worker know-how

> *We speak of the co-operative movement, especially the co-operative factories raised by the unassisted efforts of a few bold "hands." The value of these great social experiments cannot be overrated. By deed instead of by argument, they have shown that production on a large scale, and in accord with the behests of modern science, may be carried on without the existence of a class of masters employing a class of hands; [using only] associated labor plying its toil with a willing hand, a ready mind, and a joyous heart.*[62]
>
> *Inaugural speech of the International Association of Workers, October 21, 1864, London*

Throughout our research we collected numerous anecdotes about workers' ability to do tasks that were supposedly beyond them. The documentary for Canadian television on which we were working was originally going to be called "Fire the Experts." The title was meant to reflect this society's desire to get rid of the know-it-alls who put so many people into extreme poverty for their own benefit.

In Argentina's case, these supposed experts presented our problems as a sort of enigma to which there was only one solution that only a handful of people could understand or implement. This allowed technical experts and government officials to do (or undo) whatever they liked for their own benefit. An extreme example was the administration of President De La Rúa, who surrounded himself with a mind-boggling amount of ineptitude,

---

[62] Translator's note: Translation taken from http://www.marxists.org/archive/marx/works/1864/10/27.htm.

and who never tired of announcing that his solutions were the only ones. Reality, however, showed that all he did was make our problems – and our choices – worse. The quintessential Argentine example, however, is the ever-insistent Minister of the Economy, Domingo Cavallo. He continually presented his measures in different administrations with an air of supreme technical know-how, but all he ever did was sink the country further into a quagmire of economic despair.

The example of the worker-controlled factories is showing that much of this knowledge, which is supposedly out of the reach of the rest of us, can actually be replaced easily by daily experience, will, and humility. The way workers wage their daily battles leaves many professionals (and intellectuals) perplexed, and feeling that their role is now in question. As one researcher has said:

> Self-revelation is rarely considered to have "scientific" value. On the contrary, sociologists are educated for just the opposite: to be as reserved and uninvolved as possible, for fear that some hint of subjectivity might creep in.[63]

So even when presented with the evidence, the supposed experts continue to deny the possibility that workers can successfully operate a business. For example, Luiggi Zanón and the lawyer for the Brukman brothers are insistent on this.

Common sense and knowledge gained from experience are what enable a general coordinator who never finished high school to successfully manage a factory with 310 workers. The same things empower an electrical technician who presides over a cooperative that has reached its productive capacity and intends to double that capacity in a year and a half. He claims to use a shopkeeper's logic: "Buy at two and sell at three." Something similar happens among the media team at Zanón, as Carlos Guerra told us:

> They tell us we show a lot of initiative in media relations. We want to be in the newspaper every two weeks. For example, we've been in the *Río Negro* newspaper more than 400 times. They tell us that what really amazes them is our initiative and creativity. That gives you the same push you use to keep from falling victim to the struggle. We've realized that we can do it. For example, I studied engineering through the third year. They tell you that if you don't study, you can't do anything. But there are writers who didn't finish grade school, and are great.

But there are fields of knowledge that are, strictly speaking, technical, and yet still within the reach of the recovered factories. One example among many is that of IMPA. There, the workers developed their own recycling

---

[63] Mills, 1969.

system when they realized they couldn't buy small quantities of steel at a reasonable price from the monopoly (ALUAR) that controls most of the steel sales in Argentina. The workers had to work with a model that engineers had repeatedly rejected: recycling aluminum. After several tests, they developed steel that met the same quality standards as the previous supply.

There's also the case of the new ceramics being produced at Zanón from a material they named "Worker." When we spoke with Chicho, one of the workers at Zanón laboratory, he told us:

> They always kept the worker down this way: if you're not an engineer, if you're not an intellectual, then you don't know what you're talking about. But if you take a look, the factories are being run by the ones they said didn't know what they were talking about – whether they have a boss or not. They operate because we workers make them operate. And just like everything, the more we got into it, the more we learned. An engineer knows the theory, which we don't have, but we have the experience. We make theory out of our experience. We don't just throw a few things together and out comes some kind of product. We're testing and learning. We have people who help us and quality control makes sure that everything is done right. In the lab, we have a master workman (I suppose you'd call him), a chemical technician, a marketing expert and an electrical technician. They all graduated from a technical high school.

Little by little, the workers are gaining confidence in themselves. This transforms them and lets them build their own present, something they are better able to do than when they surrendered decision-making to those who supposedly knew more. Their struggle has made them suspicious of the many people, on the Right and the Left, from the government or from neighborhood groups, who either want something from them or come to give opinions on what they are doing. Generally, most of the workers seem to be impervious to these approaches, trusting only each other and prepared to coordinate only with close associates. Agustín Tosco, a *Peronista* union leader, explained back in 1959 about why the working class did not trust the employers:

> The people are asked to trust, because without trust, nothing can be done. And the people do not trust. However, this mistrust is not an innate part of their make-up, but rather a consequence of the fact that today they are told one thing and tomorrow something entirely different happens.[64]

Four decades later, these words still ring true.

Prejudice about workers' capabilities is one of the struggles that recovered factories will have to face to reach social consensus. It is striking that the countless bankruptcies and the fraudulent acts by employers have not generated the

---

[64] Lannot, Jorge, et al., 1999.

kinds of criticism and suspicion leveled at the workers. Certainly, the struggle will be long, but it's a good bet that the idea that workers can do it will take root in society. Either way, the recent crisis in Argentina helped to show that whether they can do it or not, they have little choice but to try.

3.2. Recovered legislation

> *I'm an ignorant one,*
> *and I know I don't count for much*
> *I'm the hare or the hound,*
> *according to how things go*
> *But I think those who rule us*
> *should look after us some.*
>
> Martín Fierro *by José Hernández*

Before plunging into the specific legal problems involved in the recovery of factories, let's touch on a question posed earlier by Dr. Kravetz. According to him, there is a disconnect between, on the one hand, the law as a body of established norms with a supposed societal consensus and, on the other, the actual array of forces that exists between and among social actors. As a researcher from the Labor Studies Workshop (Taller de Estudios Laborales) put it,

> In capitalist society, the law should essentially address the relation of forces between classes and social sectors. Those norms that do not reflect these relations, either directly or indirectly, cannot be applied.[65]

When laws lose contact with the reality that gives them a reason to be, they can't be applied as was originally intended, and they lose their function of legitimizing social injustice.

It's interesting to note that workers, who are sometimes seen as revolutionaries and sometimes as delinquents, mostly just want the the laws to be enforced – the same laws that are so often broken by their bosses. Employers repeatedly failed to pay taxes, or took out loans (usually from the State, and often for amounts larger than the value of the business itself), or didn't pay salaries or benefits, etc. These very same employers now present themselves as defenders of legality, talking about legal uncertainty and violations of the constitutional rights of private property. At the same time, they conveniently forget to mention tax evasion, the emptying of accounts, and other such blatantly illegal acts. Clearly, the systemic lack

---

[65] Pérez Crespo, Guillermo, 1/2003.

of respect by all parties for the law means that the law loses its reason for being. This ends up legitimizing violations of the law:

> A norm set out within the framework of a particular type of social relations constitutes a positive right that is in effect as long as that social relation exists. Once changes within society attain a certain depth and solidity, and social relations are changed or reversed, there will be enormous resistance to the application of the norm, and over time, practice will undermine the law.[66]

This is what happens with the workers in the recovered factories, when the law can't give them a satisfactory answer. They start to force the issue, just as their former employers did – with one major difference: their purposes are conspicuously more noble and respectable. This is how workers stop believing that the law is something they can use to fight for what they consider right. They become willing to bend it and force it to adapt. Examples include the expropriation law, which was not originally intended for this kind of case, nor in a broader sense for the use of cooperatives. The workers demand that laws like the bankruptcy law be changed, and may even challenge the State's monopoly on violence by resisting eviction.

This struggle questions the workings of a system that allow such unimaginable abuse to make one wonder if our society is rooted in common sense at all. Our social contracts themselves are called into question, including aspects as basic (and thus unimpeachable) as private property. True, most do so from within a capitalist logic, accusing the owners of not being satisfied with laws written for their benefit and of breaking them to tip the balance even further in their favor. However, it's not improbable that such thoughts could lead to deeper questions, even perhaps the "naturalness" of giving private property privileges to the detriment of the common good. As the philosopher Ernst Tugenhat says (and this can be applied to other implicit social assumptions), "What the classic liberal has forgotten is that property is a social institution." In other words, it is society that must be respected, and as such, society can question and denature property, reversing the conditions under which it is accepted.

> A society of private property is not based on an implicit contract among property owners. Rather, if we keep the contract metaphor, it is based on an implicit contract between owners and non-owners, and it is this unequal contract that government is expected to enforce.[67]

Another good example of the disconnect that can exist between legislation and reality is the right to work, the regulation of which has more

---

[66] Ibid.
[67] Tugenhat, Ernst, 1998.

to do with those who already have work, not the unemployed. The State and the justice system are unable to deal with fraudulent factory closings, even those in flagrant violation of the law, and respond by resorting to repression, persecution and imprisonment, which in turn further delegitimizes the system and encourages more people to ignore the law. To make the situation even worse (and further erode the workers' respect for the law), those judges who do act in good faith continue to see the world through the prism of their legal tools. In that world, conduct outside the law must be repressed in the interest of the common good. The eviction of the Brukman workers on April 21, 2003, and the subsequent posting of a police guard around the factory, is a good example of this. Brukman's lawyer explains it this way:

> From my point of view as a magistrate, there was a judicial order, it was carried out, and it continues to be carried out. As citizens, we have to accept a judge's order, just as in any other part of the world, whether it is legitimate or not. It must be respected. This is not about employment or unemployment.

Victor Turquet, of INAES and Yaguané, says that this shortcoming on the part of judges is something that he has to face all the time:

> The problem is the judicial mentality. We deal with a judge in the cases of Yaguané, El Palmar, Baskonia, Siglas, Brukman... I can't say she's a bad person. She's a fair person. But she speaks to you from an altar. She attends a multilateral meeting on Yaguané where there are twelve legislators, and asks, "Who's a lawyer?" Four people raise their hands. She says, 'Come in, please. The rest of you, wait out here." It's a challenge to make someone with that sort of mentality see reason. It's an accomplishment just to agree – after three years – that it's better to have factories that are working rather than factories that are closed and workers loitering on the street. I can bring 200 people to her door to give her a hard time, but I can't change that kind of mentality.

When judges do not take into account the unemployment and injustice with which people live, the justice system distances itself even more from people's reality. In a way, this invites the victims to ignore the legal system as they try to get what they consider fair:

> In "law as resistance," workers must question the legitimacy of that legal order. Accepting it means accepting strict limits to social protest and to the right to life itself. Certainly this kind of rupture is not simple, and in each particular case, the workers must do a careful analysis of the issues in dispute, the balance of power, the possibilities and the most effective ways of confronting an unfair law. They must use the law as tool of resistance.[68]

---

[68] Peréz Crespo, Guillermo, 01/2003.

The workers' lawyers use the law as a tool, but generally don't accept its limitations. They turn out and support labor demonstrations, when necessary. Such demonstrations of strength alone can't overcome State repression, but the symbolic value of workers confronting police with their bare hands can help shake up the tidy, balanced world in which judges and legislators seem to live.[69] Lawyers usually seem, even to the workers, to be the ones who get the goods, but in reality the success of the lawyers in most cases depends, paradoxically, on the workers' willingness to go beyond what the law prescribes.

As Mariana Salomón, a lawyer from the Centro de Profesionales por los Derechos Humanos (Professional Center for Human Rights) who is helping the Brukman workers, explains:

> We're helping the workers in the struggle to win their cases. The conventional function of a lawyer is to objectively explain to the workers which measures are legal and which are not. We propose something more democratic, that they decide in assembly what they want to do, and then we explain to them the risks involved. For instance, in the case of Brukman, from the perspective of bourgeois legality, it was against the law to occupy the factory and begin operating it again.[70]

It's very important to keep this context in mind to find explanations which may be somewhat unconventional, but clearly deeper. This explains the unusual way the workers use the laws to fight for control of their jobs.

3.2.1. Legal instruments

> *If I'm ordered to use force, I have to follow orders. If I don't, I'll end up down here beating a drum with you.*
>
> – *The Police Commissioner of Marcos Paz, June 23, chatting with workers.*

By now, it should be clear that the decision to occupy factories comes from a series of social and individual needs that leave workers no other choice. The challenge is not just to build the physical strength to resist direct attacks from other elements in society, but also to find a legal framework that permits the factories to operate legitimately – not just morally, but lawfully. This would allow the workers to fully devote themselves to producing instead of constantly resisting. In other words, even if they're ready to put up a fight against the law, the cost of resisting repression is too

---

[69] Lavalán workers battling against riot police with shields and helmets present a stark image of this kind of struggle in the documentary film "Laburantes," by Carlos Mamud, Patricia Digilio and Nora Gilges.

[70] Quoted from statements in Chaves, María et al., 2002.

high to be viable in the long term (Zanón may be the only lasting exception to this rule).

The challenge facing the lawyers who represent the workers is to find
a legal framework that meets the workers' need to occupy, resist, produce
and sell the fruits of their labor in a business that, for whatever reason,
couldn't stay open in the hands of the owners. The methods are different
in each case, including struggles that go on outside existing laws, and those
that demand new ones (like the Brukman and Zanón cases, which will
be described soon). As a lawyer used to dealing with workplace recovery
explained to me:

> There are lots of ways to legalize these factories. One of the best-known is ex-
> propriation, which many legal experts find questionable. An alternative is paying
> royalties, or rent, to the owners or to the bankruptcy court. Then the judge lets
> you keep working, like what happened at Induspel, Chilavert and the Commu-
> nications Institute. There are also cases where the owner simply sees he can't
> keep the business going, and he gives the shares and the goods to the workers.
> In Rosario, there was a factory that went up for auction, and the workers bought
> it on credit. The bankruptcy law is no good. That's why you use expropriation.
> That's the truth of the matter. It leaves you no way out. The bankruptcy law
> says if you declare bankruptcy you have 120 days to liquidate – sell it all and
> pay what you can. And what can you do with that? So, you go outside the bank-
> ruptcy law. All there is outside the bankruptcy law is the expropriation law.

So, within the current system, lawyers look for a way to reach the
goal in the best way possible, even though they themselves admit it's not
necessarily the best way imaginable. Thus far the result has been a flexible
policy making the most of the legal tools available.

That's what's happened, for example, with the use of co-ops. INAES
(the National Institute of Associationism and Social Economy), where co-
ops must register to gain legal recognition, was once a backwater institution, but nowadays everyone who wants to be his own boss signs up there.
The functionaries got impatient with the scant understanding people had
of cooperative principles, and began giving courses and doing studies to
see if co-ops in formation were really going to function as such. In general,
the workers didn't take kindly to this, because they saw these principles as
just one more source of trouble.

Victor Turquet, who is both a member of the Yaguané Cooperative and
the head of the department of INAES dealing with recovered factories,[71]
told us that some cooperatives don't look forward to visits by inspectors
from the Institute. Also, the law on cooperatives doesn't really reflect the
way recovered factories are organized, which causes friction with INAES.

---

[71] This sector, called the Executive Unit for the Recovery of Businesses in Crisis, was formed
during the Duhalde government to work with Yaguané.

To get around the obstacles in their path, the workers look for shortcuts and share experiences that others can imitate. They can't use tools that weren't meant for situations like the one in which they find themselves. You might say this intense trial and error, while traumatic at first, allowed them to discover the best ways to deal with each case, and in a way, establish a precedent that others may later use. Anyhow, the objective now is to have an active attitude towards getting legislation that fits the workers' needs and is based on the rich experiences of their struggle.

Expropriation has more than a few limitations, and as we'll see later, there's a whole litany of objections to it. For example, the laws that actually trigger an expropriation only come into effect when the same government that passed the laws pays the indemnity. If the money does not appear within the two years the State has to pay, the expropriation must be renewed. This, however, can only be done once.

The Yaguané meatpacking plant, currently run by the Yaguané Meatpacking Cooperative (Cooptrafiya), was granted an expropriation extension, and has to hurry through the steps of making the payment and deciding how it will return the money to the State. In this case, as Víctor Turquet, explains,

> There were provincial legislators who would tell you, "All right, you've got the expropriation, but there's no money. We've passed the expropriation law, and given you an umbrella. Use that to protect yourself from the 'debris,' and keep working, and after two years we'll either give you an extension on the expropriation or you'll have to get another tool."

The judge and the trustee might or might not throw "debris" at the workers, who protect themselves as best they can with their "umbrellas." But if there are obstacles in their path, things will be harder for the workers, and they'll have a harder time starting production. This is uncharted territory, with only a few more-or-less accepted legal routes, and as a result, each case is unique. For example, the Mil Hojas Cooperative, a pasta factory in Rosario, was paying a rental fee of AR$2000 a month to the court, but by June they had gathered up the AR$73,000 they needed to buy the building. That's why the following analysis of the laws used as a framework doesn't spend much time looking at specific cases. Lalo, of MNER, destroyed any hope I had of arriving at a definitive explanation:

> The reality is that you won't be able to figure out all the legal twists and turns, because here, they can invent whatever they want. Someone might be able to describe the legal framework for you at the moment, but by the time they finish, it's changed. Sadly.

That's why several bills intended to resolve this kind of conflict have already been put before the House of Deputies. One would give legal status to factories occupied during labor conflicts; another would prohibit stripping assets from businesses (which is often done with the complicity of representatives of the law); yet another would create a fiduciary fund, etc.

Perhaps the best example of the legal chaos that the lawyers face can be seen in the case of the BAUEN Hotel. In this instance, the real estate belongs to one person and the building to another. One of them is bankrupt and with huge debts. These debts were accumulated using the building as collateral, despite the fact that the building had already been sold. As if that wasn't enough, the Legislature refused to expropriate the building temporarily (which would have cost about AR$150,000 a month) or permanently (for AR$30 million, which the workers would then have had to pay), because signing off on such an expropriation would have meant mortgaging its own political future. So, for this particular case the idea emerged of renting the building from its supposed owner. In a meeting in August, one of the workers said that, while it certainly wasn't an ideal solution, it would at least let them start working, something they desperately needed to do. Diego Kravetz, lawyer for the MNER, supported this, saying, "Each cooperative does what it can. If we start being dogmatic, we'll lose a lot of businesses."

To understand how all these bankruptcies came about, we need to explain the beginning of this mess. A good part of the recovered factories have their roots in the last reform of the bankruptcy law. This reform allowed assets to be stripped from bankrupt businesses, with no one held responsible. During a meeting at the BAUEN Hotel, attorney Kravetz explained how the Bankruptcy Law was modified in 1995:

> When the law governing bankruptcy was modified, the issue of fraudulent bankruptcy was taken out. In other words, they were saying, "Go ahead, destroy your business. You have our permission. Even if you wanted to save it, you couldn't, so here's your consolation prize. Off you go – you have impunity to do what you like, because there's no more fraudulent bankruptcy." That's what happened, and in the middle of it all were the workers, who had to find this new way to struggle, which I think goes far beyond any one factory that we work with. I think we're fighting for a different model for the country, because the model they're imposing on us is a de-industrialized country, and we're fighting for an industrialized country. Later, how far the workers want to take this fight, if they want to create a different system – that's for the workers to decide. We'll see. But for now, at least as far as I can tell, what you see is a project for a country without industry: marginalization, poverty, violence, and the lack of the dignity that only work gives.

That's why one of the main demands of the MNER is the modification of the bankruptcy law.

It might be best, then, to take a quick look at the laws that affect the better part of the businesses now under worker control. It's a tricky subject, but an important part of the process, and it'll help us understand just what the workers are living through. Many didn't have enough to support their families even before this crisis began. The bureaucratic procedures seem interminable if you count the hours and minutes, or watch legislative bills or court cases come and go. It's always two steps forward, three steps back. So, to gain a deeper understanding of this phenomenon, you need to flip though at least a few pages of the legal labyrinth facing lawyers and workers when a factory is recovered. This goes beyond a normal understanding of the law. As a person connected to the movement told me:

> Not just any lawyer can get involved here. You need to know a lot, be very creative and be very, very involved in this matter – emotionally committed.

The National Constitution

The National Constitution is the basis for all our national and provincial laws. Lawyers frequently use it as the cornerstone of their arguments. Articles 14 and 14bis are of particular importance for us, because they establish, among other things, the right to work.[72]

Florencia Kravetz, a lawyer with MNER, uses the National Constitution as a basis for her arguments as often as she can:

> Another article I use a lot when I present before judges is Article 16, which talks about equality before the law. I think it's the basis for all this, because there you

---

[72] It can't be said enough times: Article 14 – All inhabitants of the Nation enjoy the following rights in accordance with the laws which regulate their use; namely, the right to work, and to engage in any legal industry; to navigate and to engage in commerce; to petition the authorities; to enter, remain in, travel in and exit from Argentine territory; to publish ideas in the press without prior censorship; to use and to dispose of one's property; to associate for useful purposes, to freely worship, to teach and to learn.

Article 14bis – Work in its different forms shall enjoy the protection of the laws, which shall guarantee the worker dignified and equitable labor conditions; a limited work day; paid rest and vacation time; fair remuneration; an adjustable minimum wage; equal pay for equal work; a share in company earnings with control of production and collaboration in management; protection from arbitrary dismissal; stability for public employees; free and democratic union membership by simple inscription in a special registry.

Labor associations are guaranteed: the right to convene collective labor meetings; to use settlement and arbitration; the right to strike. Worker representatives shall enjoy the guarantees necessary to fulfill their functions as union officials and those related to their job security.

The State shall provide social security benefits, which shall be integral and inalienable. In particular, the law shall establish: obligatory social security, which shall be in the charge of national or provincial entities which have financial and economic autonomy, and administered by the interested parties with State participation, though overlapping payments are prohibited; adjustable retirement pensions; full protection of the family; defense of family well-being; family economic compensation and the right to decent housing.

have certain rights that are guaranteed in the Constitution, and are even superior to the Constitution. If you recognize the creditors' rights, then you also have to recognize that the workers have an even greater right to their work. And I base this on Article 16. If you recognize one party's right, you have to recognize the other's.[73]

As far as the expropriations themselves go, the most important section is Article 17 of the National Constitution, which says:

> Private property is inviolable and no inhabitant of the Nation can be deprived of it except as defined by law. Expropriation for reasons of public utility must be determined by law with prior indemnity.

In other words, although private property is inviolable, the Constitution does not rule out the possibility of expropriation with indemnity. We'll see, however, that in certain cases the indemnity may be paid after the fact, and that, in practice, it's almost never paid – at least not at the time of the writing of this book.

Mariano Pedrero, a lawyer for the Zanón workers, described how judges have responded to arguments about workers' right not to accept the closure of a factory that, as the explanation went, has always operated thanks to loans from the community:

> They get angry because they don't know how to answer. They start talking about private property, and our Constitution, and Article 17 that talks about private property, and blah, blah, blah. But we answer that Article 17 of our Constitution says that we have the right to work, and that starts a pretty heavy discussion.

Since these rights are found in the National Constitution, the provinces also have to allow for the possibility of expropriation. However, the shared legal framework doesn't mean that expropriation is done in the same way in all provinces. As many of the people involved in the recovered factories have said many times, the political means to effectively make them happen currently only exist in the city and province of Buenos Aires (apart from a few exceptions, like the Renacer Cooperative (formerly Aurora Grundig) in Tierra del Fuego, or the Sieme Cooperative, a quarry in Entre Ríos, as of the beginning of August 2003). There are plenty of cooperatives in the interior, in particular in Córdoba and Santa Fe, that pressure their provincial legislatures to also support this kind of process. The lack of attention from the authorities is due, in large measure, to the links between politicians and local business people, many of whom are used to doing business

---

[73] Article 16 – The nation of Argentina admits no advantage of blood or birth. There is, in this fact, neither personal privilege nor noble titles. All its inhabitants are equal before the law and admissible to all jobs without any conditions other than capability. Equality is the basis of taxation and of public office.

thanks to this relationship. That's why, in other provinces, the most fre-
quent kinds of solutions are a little different – for example, purchase at
auction with credit, or ceding shares to the cooperative.

The Bankruptcy Law

During a meeting of recovered businesses, attorney Kravetz of the
MNER explained:

> Anyone who reads the bankruptcy law can see it's intended for liquidating a
> business, whether viable or not, in four months. That's the basic thrust of the
> bankruptcy law, which has 300 articles, it says that a judge who doesn't liquidate
> in four months is not doing his job. In other words, the idea is to tear down, to
> destroy.

Let's analyze what the Bankruptcy Law (No. 24.522) says. Article 21
explains:

> Starting preventive bankruptcy proceedings results in:
>
> 1. Laying out before the bankruptcy judge all asset claims against the debtor.
> 2. Barring presentation before the bankruptcy judge of any expropriation pro-
>   ceedings and proceedings based on family relations.

That means the law precludes any claims against expropriated goods.
The former owner of the goods can only petition the State for their value,
not the goods themselves, a provision which protects the workers against
future lawsuits against the State.

Articles 186 and 187 say that:

> ...the trustee may declare that a rental agreement or any other contract applies to
> the assets, as long as they do not dispose of the property totally or partially and
> do not exceed the time limit provided for in Article 205.

The time frame is four months, with the possibility of one 30-day extension, if that's what the judge decides. That means the workers can offer
rent to the judge to keep producing during that time.

Articles 198 and 190 also talk about continuity of production, which
has to be evaluated by the trustee, who can authorize the workers to keep
operating as long as said production does not present an obstacle to the
bankruptcy proceedings. In practice, what happens is that some judges are
prepared to grant the workers a longer continuity if they pay into the bankruptcy fund. This is a risky move, because they can be accused of not ad-
hering to the letter of the law. Once again, the issue depends on the judge's
interpretation. Article 190, modified in April 2002, specifically says that:

In the continuity of production, consideration shall be given to the formal application of the workers who depend upon production and who represent two-thirds of the active personnel, or of worker-creditors who will be actively working during the period of continuity, organized as a worker cooperative. [...] The judge, for the purposes of the present article and within the framework of the powers granted by Article 274, may provide a well-founded extension to the time limits of the continuity of the business provided for by law, to a reasonable degree to guarantee the liquidation of each establishment as a commercial entity in use.

In May of 2002, that article was used to stop the auction of Optica San Justo when the auctioneer was already in the building. While the workers stopped the bidders from entering, a petition was submitted to the judge in charge of the case, notifying her that a change to the bankruptcy law had been approved in April and that the workers had made twenty hearing requests, and that she had not replied to a single one. INAES made a strong case for the viability of the project and asked that Article 190 be applied. The judge had to stop the auction. Victor Turquet, who helped make sure Article 190 was applied, recalls:

A contract of restitution was signed, and the money went into the bankruptcy case. After twenty days, a continuity was granted, and they're working there now. It isn't a perfect instrument, but if you know how to use it...

Attorney Florencia Kravetz is more skeptical about the power of Article 19 to ensure continuity for recovered businesses:

The problem is that Article 190 was approved under a certain degree of pressure. It doesn't provide deadlines or a solid legal base, so it's not a very good tool. Without these things, certain judges won't take it into account. Still, when you can use it, you do.

This law also specifies the order in which funds for paying debts must be used – in other words, for paying the creditors who have claims in the bankruptcy proceedings. Once the assets of a bankrupt business are liquidated, the order of payment is: lawyers, trustee expenses, court fees. If there is anything left, it is distributed among privileged creditors: mortgage holders, creditors holding mortgages on goods, and labor creditors, which is to say, workers who are owed salaries, benefits etc. At the very end come unprivileged creditors, or unsecured creditors, in legal terms. It's pretty clear what the chances are of workers getting a part of what they're due. Most judges refuse to accept workers' claims as part of the purchase price of a business when a cooperative wants to buy it, which is a very difficult barrier to overcome.[74] Sometimes workers have decided not to struggle for

---

[74] As we were finishing this book, a judge accepted labor claims from a new worker cooperative as part of the purchase of the Córdoba newspaper *Comercio y Justicia*. This decision offers hope

worker control in the hopes that if the bankruptcy case ends in an auction, they'll be paid their indemnity. Realistically, this is a very remote possibility, because the amount of money auctions usually bring in is far less than the debts.

Once the expropriation is completed, the judge in charge of liquidating assets should have nothing more to do with the recovered business, since it's no longer under the jurisdiction of the bankruptcy court. In some cases, judges do stay in contact, but only when there's some particular problem.

Expropriation Laws

Expropriation is a legal mechanism by which the State appropriates something for a particular purpose. It's being used to recover workplaces. The National Law on Expropriation (No. 21.499) dates from 1948, and has been used, for example, to force property owners to sell land that was in the way of projected freeways in the city of Buenos Aires. Article 1 of this law states that:

> Public utility, which must serve as the legal basis for expropriation, encompasses all cases in which satisfaction of the public good is sought, whether of a material or spiritual nature.

The use of expropriation under this article to return jobs to a handful of workers is legally questionable, as we'll see below. Article 4 of the same law is even more specific about which cases it should be applied to:

> All assets suitable or necessary for the satisfaction of the public good, whatever their legal nature, whether they belong to the public domain or private domain, whether they are things or not, may be the object of expropriation.

To the extent that work is a right, whatever is necessary to make that right a reality can be considered a social good. This means the factories are subject to expropriation, according to some legal experts, though others reject this argument. The State has to pay an indemnity to the owners or to the bankruptcy court for the expropriation. In some cases, the expropriation is temporary, and the State makes a rental payment (usually symbolic) to the owners or to the receivership, as happened in the cases of Chilavert and Unión y Fuerza. In other cases, the law gives the workers a time limit to pay the indemnity; in the case of FORJA (Law of the Province of Buenos Aires 13.076), the term is between 10 and 20 years. If the indemnity is not paid within two years of the declaration of

---

for other cases. It would seem that the phenomenon of worker control is creating, and at the same time improving, the conditions that in turn bring about its own growth.

expropriation, the expropriation expires and must be renewed, which can only happen once.

On indemnity, Article 10 says:

> Indemnity covers only the value of the physical asset and damages that are a direct and immediate consequence of the expropriation. No consideration shall be given to circumstances of a personal nature, sentimental value, mortgage income or any potential increase in the value of the asset brought about by the expropriation. There shall be no payment for loss of profits.

On the other hand, the indemnity payment (the money going to person or group that is being "expropriated") must be a "fair price" (appraised value), as determined by the National Tribunal of Appraisals. As we'll see, in many cases, the appraised value is much higher than the auction value (which is commonly about 30% of the appraised value). This ends up making expropriation a good deal for the former owner, and is something that workers looking at expropriation should analyze carefully.

Let's look at an example. Before the FORJA expropriation decision was handed down, Lalo explained:

> This issue is easy to understand. I'll give you the example of FORJA. In our case, the appraised value is AR$2,000,000, but the auction value is AR$419,000. The State has two years to pay the appraised value to the creditors. If the owner hasn't been dispossessed, he can manage the funds together with the trustee, which is pretty risky, considering he's the one who bankrupted the business in the first place. Once the expropriation has been decided, the workers can arrange a time frame to repay the State what it disbursed. But, it doesn't always work that way. The Chilavert workers, for instance, have permission from the government of the city of Buenos Aires to use the building without paying.

Like Chilavert, the city government has granted the use of expropriated factories to cooperatives at the San Jorge Paper Mill, Panificación 5, and Baskonia.

As I mentioned, the indemnity paid to the owners or the receivership after a definitive expropriation can be an excellent deal. Lalo explained it to me:

> The other day I had a meeting with the Governor of the Province of Buenos Aires, Felipe Solá, and he told me that when all is said and done, we were playing into the hands of the owners, because they getting more money than if they had gone to auction. That's why we are asking for the indemnity for expropriation be set somewhere between the starting auction price and the assessed value. In our case, we arranged to pay it off in ten years.

For now, the State isn't really paying indemnities, and can't even establish the assessed value of the property. Lalo continues:

There's no budget for the expropriations being processed now. The Office of the Treasurer receives a dossier with the purpose of making an appraisal. The treasurer asks for a report from the Ministry of Economic Affairs on what sort of earmark is available in the budget to pay this particular expropriation. The ministry replies, "There's nothing in the budget." The treasurer says, "We can't appraise the property." That's because the appraised value is not permanent. The bureaucratic muddle makes it very difficult to get a title. At FORJA we managed to get an expropriation decision that stipulates the form of payment and the time frame, neither of which appeared in other expropriation decisions.

On indemnity, the law states that in cases of common expropriation the indemnity must be paid, or a deposit made to the judge in charge of the case, before transfer of the property. According to Article 22,

> In the case of real estate, the expropriator must give a deposit to the judge corresponding to the amount that the National Tribunal of Appraisals has determined to that effect. When this deposit has been made, the judge will award possession of the asset.

The State may, however, cede the asset to the workers through some particular disposition.

Section VIII of the same law covers uncommon expropriation in certain circumstances:

> Irregular expropriation shall proceed in the following cases:
>
> a) When, a law having been passed declaring an asset to be of public utility, the State takes possession of that asset without having paid the corresponding indemnity.
>
> b) When, for the purposes of the law declaring public utility, the asset or property shall be determined to be indisposable, due to the evident difficulty or impediment in disposing of it under normal conditions.
>
> c) When the State imposes upon the title-holder's right to an asset or object any undue restriction or limitation causing injury to his or her right to property.

Workers organized in cooperatives can take advantage of the terms of this article, which allows the State to take possession of an asset before payment of the indemnity.

Article 28 states that:

> No action on the part of third parties may impede the expropriation or its effects. The rights of the claimant are considered transferred from the object to its price or to the indemnity, the object remaining free of any encumbrance.

In other words, no creditor or specially privileged party can hinder the execution of the expropriation that has been decided by law. The only grounds for claims come from the size of the sum itself and the time limit for payment of the indemnity, not the expropriated assets.

Provincial Laws

The law of the Province of Buenos Aires covering expropriation cases (No. 5708) is similar to the national law. They are both useful for resolving issues raised in concrete cases in one jurisdiction or the other. Article 16 of the Civil Code states in Section I:

> If a civil question cannot be resolved by the letter or by the spirit of the law, the principles of analogous laws shall be used as guidelines; and if doubt persists, the question shall be resolved by means of the general principles of law, always keeping in mind the circumstances of the case.

That is to say, if there are no specific laws indicating how to resolve the issue, other similar laws and laws that deal with related questions should be applied. This suggests that in the future, cases can be based on successful precedents that will expand the body of jurisprudence available for this type of action.

The provincial law has two articles that are worth examining. Article 22 refers to expropriation. It stipulates that the State can permit immediate use of a factory in emergency cases requiring prompt possession. So, in some decisions establishing expropriation, an emergency is declared so that the workers can begin operation without having to wait for payment of the indemnity to take effect.

Article 53 states that if an area is affected by a *force majeure* (fire, flood, earthquake or epidemic), the president or the executive branch (the governor, for example) can dispense with all legal proceedings to take possession of private goods or property. Normal legal procedure is postponed to a later date.

A legal brief prepared by Dr. Luis Caro sheds some light on this issue:

> It is my opinion that the description of *force majeure* in this article is not restrictive since there are other cases that fit completely: businesses in crisis, with production totally paralyzed; workers out of work, with no resources, no hope of finding gainful employment, and dependent on a judicial process that prevents them from returning to production for several months.

In other words, a business that is not producing in a time of crisis and unemployment can be looked upon as a disaster area, and so the State has the right and the obligation to do everything in its power to lessen the impact of the catastrophe.

Taken as a whole, the laws and various articles of the Constitution make it clear it's possible to expropriate factories in cases of both receivership and bankruptcy. In some businesses, such as Crometal, it's not even necessary to reach those stages, because a lock-out was declared before bankruptcy proceedings began. In spite of that, expropriation was achieved.

3.2.2. The validity of the expropriations

As I discussed earlier, the methodology of the expropriations has been questioned by some experts, constitutional scholars, and also by parties on the Left, who believe the real struggle is elsewhere. First, let's summarize the positions of those who have doubts about the expropriations from a legal viewpoint.

The argument against using the expropriation law in a given case is supported by the equality of all people before the law. If workers ask for a special law to let them to keep working, even because of the right to work or an economic emergency, then why shouldn't the same thing apply to thousands of other cases? Obviously, the State would not be up to such a task, simply as a matter of resources, not to mention resistance from business and political forces. Public utility is limited to a group of people, or, at best, those around them, such as family members, suppliers, clients, etc. As a member of MNER explained to me,

> The problem is really that you're creating social equality. You're starting from enormous social inequality – a system that created great inequality, and people who have nothing. The thing is, you're not just talking about one business with fifty guys living in poverty. You have half the population of the country in this situation. But, I do think that the expropriations are a healthy thing. What's not healthy is forgetting that while you're helping fifty guys, there are millions more you're not helping. I think we need more global solutions.

This battle for more global solutions and for the construction of a larger force to make such a change possible justifies temporary solutions like expropriations.

During a chat at the BAUEN Hotel, constitutional scholar Daniel Sabsay explained the need to change the bankruptcy law, which had been changed during the reign of neoliberalism in our country. According to him:

> The bankruptcy law says the legislature must provide whatever is necessary for human development, for economic progress with social justice, for the productivity of the national economy, for job creation, for professional development of workers, and for the defense of the value of our national currency. As you can see, these values are not consistent with the actual practices of the State. We need to say it's time for new legislation on bankruptcy and receivership. The current laws run counter to the goals established by the Constitution for the growth and

development of the country. This incongruity should be the starting point for a struggle to rewrite laws that impede job creation and sacrifice and humiliate workers who want to go back to their jobs, so these laws conform to the ideas in our Constitution.

Another speaker at this chat, Dr. Gustavo Ferreira, explained the difference between the right to work and the right to a job:

> What we're talking about here is whether we only have a right to work – to choose an occupation – or if there is some kind of obligation on the part of the State, under certain circumstances, to provide a solution to controversial social problems.

In Ferreira's opinion, the present system of expropriations should be replaced by what he calls "normal temporary occupation," which is similar to a concept in Italian law.

Another series of questions comes from the political Left. Some of these parties, primarily the Polo Obrero[75] and the Partido de Trabajadores por el Socialismo (PTS), agree that the means of production must be reclaimed for the workers, but have a totally different vision for how that should happen. They don't accept the present legal framework, which they consider unjust. They propose a completely different approach: nationalization of businesses, meaning that the State would guarantee salaries and purchase the products. At first, this was the dominant point of view among the Brukman workers, and it still is at Zanón. According to this view, expropriation is insufficient, and ties the workers to the political vagaries of the moment and to a debt that is just as burdensome as a boss.

In a study of the expropriation decisions on Chilavert and Ghelco,[76] Pablo Heller concluded that the approval of the projects "cannot honestly be called expropriation for the benefit of the workers." While the projects had "unquestionable merit," according to Heller, "they do not meet the needs of the nascent worker-controlled businesses."[77]

The workers do not own the assets of the factories. The properties are under "transitory occupation," which is to say, they are still in the hands of the previous owners or the creditors, and are administered by the judge or trustee in charge of the bankruptcy proceedings. The city government has to pay rent to the owners and creditors.

When the two years of "transitory occupation" are up, the owners once again take possession of the asset and can do what they like with it.

---

[75] As we'll see, the PO ended up changing its mind, relaxed its position, and managed to get expropriation for the Sasetru factory.

[76] Ghelco was the name of the business taken over by the Vieytes Cooperative.

[77] Heller, Pablo, 9/19/2002.

As the PO sees it, the Chilavert workers should measure their political forces every two years, or else buy the property. I should clarify that not all expropriation decisions work this way. Some decisions made after Heller published his article, such as the San Jorge Paper Mill, Panificación 5 and Baskonia, determined that "the property, the plant and the machinery are of public utility and subject to expropriation." They were given to the worker cooperatives at no cost. Still, the most common practice so far is for the workers to pay back the State for the indemnity it advanced. Heller continues:

> This solution compensates the owners with an unexpected windfall, which is no small sum. The expropriation turns into a brilliant maneuver for bankrupt businessman, or his creditors.[78]

The workers at the expropriated factories, on the other hand, find themselves left to their fate. They own nothing, they have no sure income at the end of the month – not even a minimum wage – and most importantly, they have no working capital.

To sum up, what the expropriation decisions achieve, most of the time, is to get the ball rolling and to some extent force the movement to strengthen itself so that, when the final battle for expropriation comes, the balance of power will be in the workers' favor. This scenario, Heller says, "was expressly admitted to by a number of deputies when they supported these two projects."

As a member of the PO, Pablo Heller proposes the following alternatives:

> The State should assume its responsibilities and ensure that all expropriated factories enjoy a minimum salary, according to law. The State should take charge of covering any difference between the monthly salary received by the workers and the minimum salary stipulated in the labor laws. The workers in self-managed factories must have the right to join a union, and to receive all the social benefits of their organization.
> A special subsidy should be given to worker-managed factories so they have the necessary funds to reopen factories and put them back to work.
> The expropriated properties should be given to the workers at no cost.
> A plan should be written up to reorient and increase the scale of each factory's production, making them privileged State suppliers, so it can address the unmet demands from hospital, schools, public departments and neediest among the population.
> Let's present this program as part of the struggle to set up a central organization of recovered factories, which will set off a national struggle against capital and the capitalist State over the nationalization of banks and the creation of a single

---

[78] Heller, Pablo, "Empresas ocupadas, gestión obrera y cooperativas," 6/20/2002, available on the Internet: http://www.poloobrero.org.ar/sindical/gestionobrera/descomposicion.htm.

State banking system that incorporates a majority of representatives from worker-managed, recovered factories, as well as elected representatives of the working class in general, on its Board of Directors.[79]

Raúl Godoy, a Zanón worker and one of the leaders of the struggle in Nequén, explained to us how he understands "nationalization," which they're pursuing at the factory:

It means that the provincial government has to guarantee supplies, salaries, electricity and gas. We are responsible for producing and for deciding together with all the other workers about the needs of the factory, how much we spend, what parts we buy, etc. That's the mechanism. We're not businesspeople. We don't want to compete in the capitalist market with other workers working in other factories. We want this to be more social, even if not forever, right? And we're fighting together with other organizations of both unemployed and employed people, but in this particular case, the factory would function with the State paying for supplies and salaries, and we would produce things and direct money to where it's needed, so the whole community knows where the money is going. We can have community control of the factory through the workers. I think if this were done on a large scale, a lot of things would change.

In short, from this perspective:

The program of the "recovered factories" raises the question of reforming the bankruptcy law and creating a fiduciary fund. Once bankruptcy is decreed, the idea is to grant the workers the management of the business for two years. [...] The MNFRT's goal is to manage microenterprises within the framework of the market and system of capitalist exploitation.[80]

Given the present legal system and the current struggles, this analysis is not outlandish. Indeed, the movements accept it as correct. Luis Caro, president of MNFRT, explained why during a meeting:

We are asking for a change in the expropriation law because, we all know that when there's an expropriation, it has a time limit, and there are cooperatives that can't make the payments – they're just too high. It's a shame for a cooperative to start production, become profitable, hold on to their jobs, and then, after two years, have to shut down because it can't meet its obligations. That's why most cooperatives need help from the authorities.[81]

From the editorial page of the MNER's magazine, Eduardo Murúa comments on the need for profound change:

---

[79] Heller, Pablo, 19/09/2002.
[80] Ibid.
[81] Abrecaminos, No. 1, December, 2002.

We are aware that what really needs to happen is to change all the laws, replace the liberal[82] Constitution with a brand new social Constitution. However, while we gather the social forces necessary for that revolutionary transformation, we support every step forward in defense of the rights of the working class [...]. We also reaffirm that with or without this law, or even outside the law, we will not allow a single job to be lost in Argentina. We will continue to unconditionally support workers who struggle to recover the factories under their control and [to prevent] the stripping of assets from those factories.[83]

There seems to be some confusion about certain organizational aspects of the cooperatives. At Zanón, for example, in the middle of important discussions, somewhat inaccurate references were made to the inequalities supposedly appearing at expropriated factories in the hands of cooperatives. Avi conducted an interview with Carlos Saavedra, the general coordinator at Zanón, and asked him why they chose nationalization as their legal framework.

Carlos Saavedra: This is my personal opinion. In this system, in this country, where there's 50% poverty, nothing that's cooperatively-run or State-run is going to work. Secondly, I don't share the views of the cooperative system because I don't agree with a system of hierarchies in the factory. That's my personal opinion. Again: equal pay for equal work. In my opinion, there shouldn't be economic differences, so we're against cooperatives on economic grounds. And in order to form a cooperative we would have to give up our rights and all my years of work. You see?

Avi: No, I don't see. They tell me that in the cooperatives everybody earns the same thing.

CS: Let me explain. In this system, with the level of poverty we have, it would never work. Secondly, forming a cooperative would force us to compete and we don't want to compete with anybody or leave anybody out on the street. Right? We want to work and earn money. We don't want to compete. We're not businesspeople. That's not our motivation. We simply want a more just society. There are places that work as cooperatives, and I'm happy for them. But in our case, at Zanón, it would never work. Of course, that doesn't mean that we can't work with the people from the cooperatives – we can.

A: Why wouldn't it work here?

CS: It wouldn't work, first of all, because it would be for two years, and because we'd be responsible for the US$75 million that Zanón owed, and we don't want to pay that, for personal reasons.

While the cooperatives as legal entities do not necessarily establish egalitarian guidelines for salaries or do away with hierarchical structures,

---

82 Translator's note: "Liberal" should be understood to mean "neoliberal."
83 "Ocupar, Resistir, Producir" magazine, MNER, N° 1, 11/30/02.

in practice the better part of them have indeed chosen to do these very things. That's even true in factories with modest political objectives, like Unión y Fuerza. The legal framework is not the defining feature of the cooperatives – in fact, the workers set up cooperatives simply because they are the most direct way to establish worker control. Then each factory develops specific types of labor relations created by the workers themselves. In the overwhelming majority, the source of all authority is the assembly. In fact, on several occasions, we heard Eduardo Murúa remark to workers that if they hired new people at lower salaries, or if they denied them the right to vote, they would no longer belong to the movement.

Returning to Polo Obrero, its ambition seems rather excessive given the current situation. It's obvious that workers suffer injustices under the capitalist system, but it's also true that not all of them can see these injustices, or that all workers think the solution is revolution. For example, one of the FORJA workers voted, with no apparent sense of contradiction, not only for capitalism but for its most rabid and exploitative form, when he cast his ballot for Menem/Romero ticket in the April 27, 2003 election.

Those that take an all-or-nothing approach when most people are more concerned about hunger than social or class consciousness find themselves alone in a political wasteland, powerless as ever. On the other hand, building power, or "counter-power," through praxis, which promotes the building of social consciousness before heading into battle, can turn out to be not only more reasonable, as MNER's leaders argue, but also more effective at achieving goals. Also, everything clearly depends on a consensus among the workers that the struggle must continue... something that is not always guaranteed.

Many of the arguments from the Left can be better understood from the points of view of its analysts.[84] The most radical elements on the Left saw signs of revolution in the "out with them all" vote in the 2001 elections, and a "...revolutionary political situation created by the popular uprising of December 19 and 20."[85] But two years later, the same Left turned a blind eye to the election of April 27, 2003, when 79% of the population cast a vote, with less than 2% of ballots blank or spoiled, and the Right emerged with a solid victory in Buenos Aires.

Nationwide, Menem's ultra-neoliberal model reaped one in four votes. One in four is a lot. "A massive popular rebellion is not a revolution," as James Petras concludes.[86] The road from actions to social consciousness is straight, but long, and there are many rest stops along the way, as shown

---

[84] Some intellectuals on the Left, such as James Petras, have an even more pessimistic reading of the situation than this one. See his paper, "Argentina: 18 months of Popular Struggle – A Balance," 5/28/2003.

[85] Heller, Pablo, April, 2003, page 63.

[86] Petras, James, "Argentina: 18 months of popular Struggle – A Balance," 5/28/2003.

by some workers who want to sit in their co-ops and not worry too much about others.

The growing social "pacification," which seems to have found its highest expression in the arrival of Néstor Kirchner as President, seems to be lulling to sleep many sectors of society that were very active a few short months ago. Upon taking office, the new President showed leadership on social issues (at least in his first months in office), and partly neutralized the popular movement, which is starting once again to dream that someone will solve their problems for them. Self-management and direct democracy are increasingly things of the past for most people. On the other hand, beyond the legitimacy of a given case, the repression at Brukman factory shows that the combative spirit of the workers and their neighbors has its limits. When they see the flags of the most radical political parties fly, even the presence of the Mothers of the Plaza de Mayo can't help them to overcome their fear, sad as it is to say.

As Naomi Klein explained during one of the round-tables in front of Brukman just after the eviction in April:

> The problem is that theories are often wrong. Sometimes the intellectual attempts to impose sense and structure are openly dogmatic, rigid, and forced, alienating the vibrant language and moments lived together. Instead of a factory where a group of people decide to hold onto their jobs and work with dignity, they imagine a pre-revolutionary cell building power to take over the State.

Coordinating pickets, assemblies and recovered factories seems more doable once there has been some minimal consolidation. Trying to get everything just right from the outset means leaving gaps at every step. One of the hypotheses of this book is that subjective change in the workers is a slow but indispensable process if profound change is to happen in society. Occupying factories, even precariously, at least creates temporary spaces where the workers can cultivate the circumstances to develop political consciousness. While there are no guarantees, this will at least give them a chance for greater combativeness and commitment to deeper goals.

The movements to which most of the factories belong are betting more or less explicitly that in two years, the workers' economic, social and political situations will have improved enough to buy them another two years. That's what happened at Unión y Fuerza and at Yaguané. The optimistic take on this would be that they are gathering strength for the final battle. On the other hand, the most radical and intransigent workers, those who want to do everything at once, are not getting anywhere, and appear to be rapidly wearing themselves out. This seems to be what's going on at Brukman, where, after nearly two years they again have to fight for expropriation, and under worse conditions than the first time.

On the other hand, the Zanón workers may not have found a legal framework for their demands (which are similar to the ones outlined by Polo Obrero), but they have been able to weave themselves social acceptance and legitimacy in Nequén, which makes them almost unbeatable, at least for the time being. Popular pressure forced the Governor of Nequén, Jorge Sosbich, a long-time acquaintance of Luiggi Zanón, to publicly announce that he would not send the police into the factory.[87] To a certain extent, the workers are making up for their lack of legal status with their social legitimacy, but this strength may weaken if society continues to demobilize.

Anyway, beyond all the critical crossfire it's good, *a priori*, that a variety of strategies develop, with the diversity meaning that at least some will find effective paths that others can subsequently follow. It's a sort of political evolution. To work, it requires complete autonomy and decentralized decision-making. In practice, the workers know that it's best for everyone to focus on what they have in common, and look past their methodological differences. That's why Luís Caro, Eduardo Murúa and workers from many other factories stood with Brukman the day the police repression came down, and left their critiques for internal discussions at a later moment.

To be sure, a good part of this discussion will probably have to be sent straight to the archives, because just after this book was finished a cooperative made up of Polo Obrero members was granted an expropriation decision for SASETRU, a business that had been closed for almost twenty years. They hope to have it working again soon, but it won't be easy, as only 20 of the 150 members of the co-op are former workers at the business and, as has been discussed previously, worker knowledge is as valuable as machinery. And speaking of machinery, what the workers found in SASETRU in August 2003 was in very bad condition.[88] So, it looks like the PO has finally accepted the fact that, with all its faults, expropriation sometimes really is the best option available.

The discussion has clearly been outrun by the facts. Perhaps we are finally seeing what Naomi Klein advised outside Brukman. Using one of those snappy English phrases, she said, "If it works, do it!"[89]

3.2.3 In practice

As I've said repeatedly, the stories in this book show how all things are relative. The practices in them are resistant to traditional patterns of rules,

---

[87] *Río Negro* newspaper, 4/9/2003, "Es un caso político, dijo Sobisch." ["It's a political case, says Sosbich."]

[88] Vales, Laura, "Fábrica con Historia," *Página/12* newspaper, 1/9/2003.

[89] May, 2003.

and are shaped instead by current events. Workers and owners are constantly arguing and exchanging strong words, usually far from lawyers in suits, where "his honor" doles out "justice," like in the movies. Day-to-day fights tend to get sorted out by constantly measuring strength against the enemy. There are many examples. Here, we'll take a look at La Vasquita, a dairy plant in Marcos Paz.

The case of La Vasquita is an example of the variety of ways to pull off an occupation and possibly an expropriation: legal ins-and-outs, bankruptcy proceedings, asset stripping, auctions, court orders, takeovers, and more. At this factory, the workers tell of how the senior partner in the business had been gradually defrauded by the two junior partners. Finally, he was unable to keep up with his loan payments and had to agree to auction off the building that housed the factory. While the auction was being finalized, the plant continued operating at a loss, and at partial capacity, until it closed its doors in the middle of 2002.

The judge in the case ordered two auctions held, but not a single offer was made. According to auction regulations, if the first two attempts to sell the property fail, the third one is held with no minimum price. That's how a politically-connected neighbor named Pedro Ragone was able to buy the factory for about AR$40,000. Since the property was assessed at AR$700,000, the new owner had gotten himself quite a bargain. The sale at the third auction happened in December, and in February the workers decided to take over the factory in spite of it all.

On June 23, 2003, workers from other factories and neighbors from around Avellaneda Park came together to defend La Vasquita from the raid scheduled for 9:30 that morning. When we got there, we learned that last-minute negotiations were going on in court, but an hour later, Carlos Monje, the president of the cooperative, arrived without an agreement. If it hadn't been for the palpable potential for violence, what happened next would have seemed picturesque: Ragone and his lawyer tried to walk up to the factory entrance, while the workers and their supporters grouped up, forming a human blockade. This all happened as the police commissioner from the nearest station watched closely, with twenty or so policemen spread out around the factory entrance, waiting for his orders.

After some pushing and shoving, Ragone and his lawyer pointed out to the police commissioner that they were not being allowed to enter the factory despite having the deed in hand. They asked him to do something about it. The moment of truth had arrived. There were some frightened faces, particularly those of the La Vasquita workers, but they weren't about to back down. I suddenly realized what scared them: unlike the judges, trustees, and businesspeople, the workers had nothing more to their names than their health and the strength of their arms. Losing this fight would mean having nothing with which to support their families – no savings, no insurance, and almost certainly, no rich relatives – and they knew it. They had to be very sure of themselves, because they may well have been risking all they had left.

The workers gathered around the police commissioner, his helpers, Pedro Ragone, his wife and his lawyer. A noisy discussion began, and opinions were exchanged from two worlds so different, they could barely understand each other. Alicia Montoya, from the "December 20" assembly (which occupied Clínica Portuguesa) in Flores, began to speak out as the representative of the MNER, in defense of the La Vasquita workers. Anecdotal as it may be, what follows is the dialogue, in nearly complete form, as it took place in front of the factory that day. The idea is to show the variety of situations in which the struggle takes place.

> Pedro Ragone: They asked me to stay here for six months and then pay rent. So then I proposed that they get another place, and I'd pay the first six months rent. And also the governor and Senator Arboleda could pay, because they say they wanted to help this business. So yesterday these people tell me they want two more months. In two months time, we'll be right where we are now. If the expropriation goes ahead – great! We'll leave the premises and you take over. But that's not going to happen.

> Alicia Montoya: Do you know Acrow Scaffolding?

> PR: Yes.

> AM: Well, the expropriation came through two weeks ago. It was done with the expropriation law. The factory is working now. Of course, it's much bigger than this place. But we're looking to do the same thing. The problem is that the legislature is backed way up, but expropriations are coming out. What the workers wanted was thirty to sixty days to give the law time to come out, a law you know perfectly well will benefit you to the extent the judge decides. The amount you're going to get from the valuation is better than the best negotiator in the world could get you. So what I'm saying is that in a country like ours, with whole families out of work, they're not looking for shortcuts. They're asking for an expropriation law, working capital and a commitment from the governor of the province to give working capital for the reclaimed factories.

> PR: So why don't they give working capital for the businesses that are still working to keep them from going under?

> AM: Well, that would be –

> PR: Because if I can get some, this place won't stay closed. I'm going to do things here.

> AM: The fact is that, today, in Argentina, there's a bankruptcy law. There's legislation that defends this process.

PR: But there was a sale here. I bought the place and I want my property.

AM: Your right is a legal right, and ours is a legitimate right.

PR: You have no legitimate right.

AM: It is a legitimate right. The right to work is above the right to profit.

PR: This is private property, and Argentina isn't a communist country yet.

AM: The right to work has nothing to do with communism, sir. The right to work has to do with survival.

PR: Well, I can't talk to you. We think too differently.

AM: What do you mean, we think too differently? I'm saying...

(They both speak at once and there is no dialogue. Finally, they calm down and we can hear Alicia again.)

AM: What I'm trying to say is that in sixty days...

PR: In sixty days we'll be right where we are today.

AM: No, because there's an agreement being signed. The *compañeros* from this co-operative are signing, and other cooperatives too. If the time runs out, and nothing has happened with the expropriation, you can go ahead and use the police.

PR: Why don't you people just leave peaceably and if the expropriation is declared we'll give it back to you. It'll be closed for two months, with nobody occupying the place. If what you say is true, and the expropriation will be resolved in two months, you could leave now and come back when there's a decision. We'll make an inventory of everything and if you don't get an expropriation in two months, the place is mine to do what I want with. In the meantime we'll be on stand-by. The factory's not operating anyway.

AM: That's not so. They're getting things going. There's a possibility of some working capital.

PR: Well, let them give you working capital for some other place that you can rent. Why do you have to have this place? I keep telling you that I'll give you a hand with the rent.

Cándido: If I had bought it for AR$20,000, I'd pay the rent too!

PR: So why didn't you come and buy it for AR$20,000? Besides, it wasn't AR$20,000.

Pitu: Yes, but the auction was challenged.

PR: But the challenge was dismissed. It wasn't submitted in time –

AM: Fine, but a property with an appraised value like the one I saw –
Cándido: The judge changed the inventory for us at Chilavert.

PR: What does the judge have to do with this? This place went up for auction three times. The first two times it didn't sell, and the third time, it sold for that price. If it had sold for more, what difference would that make?

AM: You're right, it wouldn't make any difference at all.

Pedro Ragone's wife: How many years has this place has been closed down – and suddenly you decide you want it?

PR: It's been closed for four years.

A worker: Seven months ago.

PR's wife: Seven months ago, what?

AM: Seven months ago we were producing, even if it was at a loss.

PR: With 500 liters of milk, or some ridiculous thing.

The argument went on for a while longer, and finally, Alicia went off with several workers to discuss the possibility of accepting Ragone's offer of leaving the factory closed and under guard for another month to see if they could get some sort of decision from the court in La Plata. Actually, what she had been trying to do (and you might have been able to tell from the dialogue) was buy time until the movement's lawyer arrived. As the assembled workers and police officers chatted, some kids from Parque Avellaneda practiced their almost non-existent rhythm on a variety of drums. One of the workers encouraged them: "Make some noise – things are getting too quiet here." A policeman standing nearby said, "We could start shooting." The worker replied, "No-o-o," with a laugh. I had never seen Argentina so close to becoming a Latin American cliché.

Meanwhile, I took advantage of the lull to approach Pedro Ragone for a short interview:

Esteban Magnani: What is it you intend to do with this factory?

PR: First, I'm going to fix it up so it'll be useful again. I mean, it's not going to sit empty – it's going to create jobs. And I can assure you that it will create more jobs under one owner than under six people with no capital. It's not a simple question of knowing how to produce, you also have to know how to sell. This is a tough time to try to manage a business. Marcos Paz has several dairy plants, and most of them are having trouble. And if this one went bankrupt, it's because managing it wasn't easy.

EM: The workers are saying that the factory's been stripped.

PR: Not true at all. The business has been closed for almost four years. They'll verify that at the DGI.[90] Of the six people here today, not one is an employee of the business. You can't just have an empty plant and say you're occupying it and set up a cooperative and have the province give you money. And who is the province? The province is us, the taxpayers. Look, the employees of the provincial government just had a 13% pay cut, and they're not going to get it back, because there's no money. And the government is going to spend money here? On this place that has little chance of success? I told them if they found a smaller place, I would pay the rent for six months and if other people help them with capital, all the better. Why does it have to be here?

EM: But wouldn't it be cheaper in the long run to finance this kind of project than to pay unemployment benefits to 150 workers?

PR: Financing a project like this to make it viable would cost a lot of money. Listen, if they were going to process milk here, they would need at least 7,000 liters a day. You know how much that costs? That's AR$150,000 a month for milk, and you'd need another AR$50,000 or AR$60,000 for other supplies. You'd need more than AR$200,000 a month. And then you have to sell what you make.

EM: Are you familiar with other expropriated factories?

PR: Not here in Marcos Paz. The truth is, this is the first time I've been in a situation like this. But you know why they usually manage to survive? They don't pay taxes, because people get by on less – they make less than they did before, as employees. That's the sad truth. So we're creating an economy that is poorer all the time. All around you see drivers in ramshackle cars.

EM: But that's not because of the expropriations.

PR: No, it isn't, but we're getting used to this poverty. And since there are no jobs, these people are allowed to drive around in dilapidated vehicles, and it's a danger to everyone.

EM: But not paying taxes – isn't that almost a tradition among a good part of Argentine businesspeople?

PR: No. If you're on the rolls, well, you might get a bit creative with the books, but if you don't pay your taxes, you can't operate. They send you letters constantly, and it's just impossible to function if you don't pay.

EM: I ask that because in many cases the businesses that were expropriated had not been paying their taxes or their debts and they went bankrupt, and now the cooperatives that took their places are paying their taxes.

---

[90] Translator's note: The DGI is the national tax agency.

PR: Well, in the few places I know that are working, I see people – I mean, I don't know all the details, but they're making less than before, and of course they're not paying social security, and I'm pretty sure they don't pay taxes. That's how it is with a lot of microbusinesses. The people who sell things on the street, I don't think they pay any taxes. It pains me to see these people being fooled into thinking they can do something that's really hard to do, because I don't think managing a business is easy at all.

Alícia interrupted us. She came over, followed by several workers, to ask Ragone if he would wait a few more days until a (non-existent) meeting of the provincial senate had taken place. That way, she argued, he could contemplate the truth of the expropriation and the advantages it could bring him, such as the fact that he would be paid the assessed value of the factory, which would be about 35 times what he'd paid. Ragone agreed, and after signing the appropriate papers, he shook everybody's hand and left, giving his word that he wouldn't do anything until Thursday.

Once we were inside the factory, Pitu, a journalist from the movement, told me that Ragone is well known in Marcos Paz for confiscating property from people who owe him money, that he had been a candidate for mayor and now owned a cheese-making factory, which meant La Vasquita would be useful to him. I asked Pitu how it could be that nobody had bid anything at the first two auctions and Ragone had gotten the factory at such a ridiculous price. He took the time to explain to me how auctions really work in Argentina...

Meanwhile, Alícia was complaining about having had to go out and speak, because no lawyer or anyone who knew anything about the law had managed to come to the plant. Still, in the end, she laughed and told us about the police commissioner who had said to her, "If they order me to use force, I have to use force. Otherwise I'll lose my job and I'll have to come down here and beat a drum with you." Everyone burst out in relieved laughter.

On July 14, the anniversary of the French Revolution, the workers of La Vasquita were evicted.

3.3 The recovered economy

> *If anyone thinks this is a delirious dream or a utopia,*
> *they should come and see our factory.*
>
> *Alejandro López, Zanón worker*

One of the issues that may have been skipped over in this book, or at least not discussed in much detail, is the question of the economic viability of these businesses. Obviously, recovered factories operate within a capitalist framework, and as such they must obey its laws to a certain extent just in order to be able to function. Competition is the golden rule of the market, and if the workers are able to achieve efficiency and produce quality products at a good price, there are vast possibilities for reclaimed factories to grow.

There have been cases of challenges by former owners, but, at least for now, they haven't been coordinated or systematic. When asked why the corporations are not launching a coordinated attack, the workers reply that the marketplace is a highly anarchical environment where whoever competes well wins. So far, as long as no recovered business has gotten in the way of a really powerful opponent or scared other businesspeople too badly, this seems to hold true.

However, there are exceptions, and some cooperatives have had to face off with important business groups with powerful contacts. The difficulties of recovering a factory are even more serious when these confrontations happen, but the visibility that the co-ops' struggle gives to corruption scandals would seem to invite businesspeople to avoid large-scale conflicts. By and large, the legal and political struggle hasn't spread to the economic domain in the form of boycotts.

Another explanation for the absence of corporate obstruction tactics is that, for now, these factories are just "little stands," as the workers say. If the conflicts get bigger, the whole situation will become much more complicated.

In this chapter, we'll look at the kinds of difficulties the businesses face once they've overcome the legal hurdles and the challenges of re-opening. Once they reach these objectives, they're actually able to function better than before, recovering their clientele with relative ease. As Murúa explained:

> In most cases, there's a lot of sympathy for this kind of thing, for recovering businesses, even among some capitalist clients. They are happy to buy from us and we have no problem with them. At IMPA we have clients such as Nestlé, Arcor, Fel Fort – big clients, some of them multinationals. First priority is price, and then quality. If we can provide things for the lowest price, or at least a competitive price, and still with good quality, we are guaranteed a market. We're sure about that.

From an economic perspective, most of the recovered businesses are showing sustained growth – and remember, these are places that until recently had trouble paying salaries, or sometimes even working at all. Even when the workers' shares remain low, they're usually better than the higher salaries that the old bosses sometimes paid and sometimes didn't.

Another point of no small importance is that, in a context where conventional businesses increase productivity by firing workers, most recovered businesses that have managed to achieve legal stability have quickly found themselves in need of more strong arms. That's why many leaders of the movements say that a government policy in favor of self-management, a few changes to the bankruptcy laws, and the creation of a fiduciary fund would bring the unemployment rate down significantly. These changes would let idle equipment and workers be productive again. The alternative is to keep adding to the number of workers living off unemployment benefits and sell off perfectly good equipment as scrap.

In the absence of more general statistics, let's look at some data on individual factories, most of which have been producing for a little over a year. At Lavalán, which has been working for less than a year, the workers told us they are taking home AR$1200 a month. At Chilavert, which started up at the same time as Lavalán, they went from AR$200 a month to AR$400, and then to AR$800 in six months, despite having to change the worn-out parts and, for example, fill all the fire extinguishers. At Zanón, earnings are capped AR$800 per month, which lets them reinvest and grow at 10% per month. At the Química Sur Cooperative, they've gone from 34 workers to 60. At IMPA, they make more than AR$1000 a month, sometimes far more. At Unión y Fuerza, they make at least twice what the boss paid them, and they calculate that next year, they'll make an investment that will let them double their production. On the other hand, things aren't always this way. Some factories have difficulty taking off, such as FORJA San Martín, which is looking for AR$500,000 to "get a good start," as one worker explained. At Nueva Esperanza and El Aguante, they're having serious trouble finding clients, and the members are earning very little.

Still, the evidence thus far indicates this is not part of some utopic delirium. Nearly 170 factories are operating under worker control. They're creating jobs, which is an end in itself for this type of project, and they don't collapse in the face of their first crisis the way many owners did when they saw their profits dwindling.

The economic effect these factories have had in terms of revitalizing the areas around them, particularly in smaller cities and towns, is very important. The town of Las Varillas in the Province of Cordoba is a great example of this impact. The Zanello factory, located in Las Varillas, is a mixed capital business (cooperative, State, and private) that makes tractors costing around 30% less than equivalent imported machines. There are no mechanics, welders or machinists to be had in town, because they're all busy at Zanello or in some industry supplying the factory. Since more money has come into the region, commercial activity of all sorts has been given a boost. A reclaimed factory may not have a noticeable effect on the GNP, but it can certainly transform people's lives.

While this phenomenon has had only a marginal effect on a national scale, it's useful to analyze why the more solid projects have gained strength.

3.3.1 The owner cost

*It is laudable for workers to fight to keep their jobs, even
sacrificing a good part of their salary. Because in general, they make little or nothing at the beginning, or they
get by on AR$150 from the subsidy plans for heads of
households. But things aren't that simple. These factories
stopped producing for a reason.*

Editorial by *Juan Alemán*, in the newspaper La
Razón, *3/10/03*

The expression used for the title of this section is an obvious para-
phrase of labor cost, which is the "cost" of salaries in capitalist production.
The concept of "labor cost" is not neutral, since it is normally used to
describe a variable typically considered a burden in normal businesses.
This view of the function of salaries in capitalism (as a cost) has to do with
neoliberalism, which has had such dire consequences on our society and
culture – not to mention our economy, where such policies are supposed
to be beneficial. The concept of the "Argentine cost," for example, is still
used to denounce the expectations of the workers in this country, which
are supposedly so high that they threaten the workers' own interests by
reducing the competitiveness of national industries and leading to unemployment. According to this logic, a salary is not a fair remuneration meant
for the well-being of the general population, but rather a cost that weakens
competitiveness and inhibits the growth of a business and, ultimately, that
of the economy as a whole. If workers reduced their demands, the general
economy would improve, which would in turn improve the well-being of
the population. This was the argument used in the '90s to impose work
flexibility, the benefits of which were obscured by an unprecedented unemployment rate. Once in a great while, the wealth runs over the edge of the
champagne glass, but what have mostly been socialized are persistent periods of crisis. In other words, the assumptions used to argue for the necessity of reducing labor costs appear to be based more on strategic fallacies
than solid, provable arguments. This crucial point winds its way through
this book, and with it, we will do an economic analysis of the experiences
in the recovered factories.

This section will not consider labor cost, but rather proposes to turn
the argument on its head, talking instead about the cost of the businessman.
This allows us to confront an argument heard regularly in interviews or in
articles like the one chosen for the epigraph of this chapter: "If the owner,
with all his wisdom, couldn't make it, how could the workers?" Presented
here are some of the fundamental pieces to help answer this question. The
owner cost, as proposed here, is the capitalist's need to produce a certain

amount of benefit in order to justify leaving his capital on the street – that is, to continue risking it. Within the owner cost, we could also speak of a managerial cost (at least for the highers-paid managers). Supposedly, these professionals have exclusive domain over specific knowledge; yet in the recovered factories, the workers are in charge of administrative tasks, planning, technicalities, etc. They often say in the factories that with one manager's salary, you can pay ten workers. For example, Zanón's production used to finance an office in Buenos Aires with 100 staff. It has been demonstrated that this number of people was unnecessary to make the business work, and today it is growing without their help. It should be clear that, while there are cases where managerial knowledge was beneficial, its absence does not determine success or failure. In some cases, it was a burden that impeded the growth of the business.

The workers' commitment to their daily tasks allows them to save up some money and noticeably improve the efficiency of their work, and hence, its profitability. The key variable explaining the success of these businesses, however, is the absence of the owner. To put it rather simplistically (and perhaps a bit crudely), the business doesn't need to come up with the money to let the owner buy a new car every year, pay taxes on his country estate, and send his children to private universities. The business becomes more competitive, and finds more possibilities for growth.

A satisfactory profit rate for a private enterprise, depending to some extent on the situation of a particular country, is around 10% of total income produced.[91] The rest goes into fixed and variable costs: salaries, materials, and reinvestment. For most businesspeople (within a capitalist logic, of course), if this rate of profit falls below a reasonable percentage, there would no longer be sufficient stimulus to keep the factory open. So, when faced with a crisis, businesspeople lose their motivation to continue risking their capital and must take steps to ensure their profits. This might mean making sacrifices while waiting for the situation to improve, cutting salaries, or "boosting production" by firing staff.[92] Or, as in many cases of businesses that were later recovered, they simply asked for loans that they never paid off, emptied out the business, declared bankruptcy, and eventually bought the business back at fire-sale prices and debt-free. To a greater or lesser extent, the capitalist logic of maximum profit as the highest goal legitimizes all these possibilities. The fact that the employees are out of work is just a

---

[91] This percentage may be low compared to the actual profits made – for example, by the telephone companies at the end of the '90s. Former President Menem assured them in the privatization documents that they would make a minimum of 15%. This is far above the rate earned by their predecessors.

[92] There are cases where capitalist investments have been used to pay for indemnity to fired workers. When such businesses downsize, this has an immediate effect on productivity. From this perspective, firing workers is, in a certain sense, an investment.

side effect that has no impact on the rate of profit (since they don't have to pay indemnity in bankruptcy cases), and as such doesn't factor in economic considerations. So either no one is guilty or, perhaps more accurately, the guilt is too diffused to hold anyone accountable. As a social studies professor of mine used to insist in each class, investing is the private decision that has the greatest social impact. He even went so far as to worry that it was perhaps too much responsibility to leave in the hands of a select few.

This logic of placing the maximization of benefits on the highest altar is quite different from that of a recovered business. For them, profit is expendable – or, to put it another way, it doesn't exist, to the extent that it's divided up among the variables we looked at earlier. Recovered businesses have choices regarding what to do with what we would have previously called profit: donations, social investing, or training plans. Social investing is an innovation of the recovered factories that would have been almost unthinkable within a strictly capitalist logic. That is, unless we count donations from large businesses like, for example, Microsoft to governments considering abandoning Windows,[93] or the foundations that exist either to improve the image of some corporation through the funding of social projects or to use its profits to genuinely ameliorate the effects of boundless profit: poverty, marginalization, unemployment, etc. In these cases, it's not about washing one's hands or acting in good faith. Rather, there are other considerations, like consolidating products, improving the company's image, or, to put it more pointedly, keeping a lid on the system to keep it from overheating and blowing up. The latter, of course, is not part of some macabre plan, but it does often work that way. One hand takes and the other hand gives (significantly less, of course), and this keeps the system going. As we'll see, it may be that the recovered factories, by distributing the wealth among certain social sectors but not resisting the system itself, are also keeping a lid on the system and, in a sense, allowing it to continue functioning.

There are many recovered businesses that make donations, like the Zanón workers, who gave ceramics to the Neuquén Hospital and the flood victims in Santa Fe; the Chilavert workers, who got computers so their neighbors could take classes in their factory; Nueva Esperanza, which lends its space for protest meetings, and so on. What they get from this is a fundamental change in the image of their factory – no longer a simple site of production, it takes on a social function, weaving networks, linking people.

Nor is it strange to hear about cross-loans, which are made without interest or even a commitment to repay, between recovered businesses. For example, IMPA loaned money to several businesses that were lacking the

---

[93] This occurred, for example, when the Peruvian government considered replacing the expensive Windows operating system with Linux, which is free, in its State offices.

necessary start-up capital and asked very little in return. Such acts create
a culture of cooperation between recovered businesses. This allows them
to survive, not through competition against other economic actors, but
through solidarity with other actors in the market, with other workers,
with other human beings. In the recovered factories, profit maximization
is an objective, but not the only one, or even the most important one. It's
the workers who decide the fate of this pile of money (which before was
profit), and they can do with it as they please.

There are cases where, because of hard times or structural reasons,
there may not be money above and beyond the costs of production (including salaries). The workers could never consider closing the factory,
because that would be counter to their own interests. The objective of a
recovered business is more than producing profit – it's preserving jobs. In
a worst-case scenario, the workers must reduce their own salaries to stay
competitive and keep functioning. This is something capitalists are very
unlikely to ever do to themselves, not only for economic reasons but for
social and cultural reasons as well. In our society, private property gives
them the right to make whatever decisions they want about their own well-
being without considering greater morality or the consequences to others.
In a certain sense, as Cándido from the Chilavert press said, workers have
an advantage over owners when it comes to making a business function,
and even the State has to admit as much.

Now then, from where did we say earlier that profits come? According
to a neoliberal perspective, they are the fair payment made to the capitalist for taking the risk of investing his capital. On the other hand, a
Marxist perspective says that surplus value is extracted from workers by
capitalists taking advantage of their privileged situation, which originat-
ed from an unjust primitive accumulation. This explanation is simplistic,
even within Marxism, but it's not my intention to go into the variations
and subtleties necessary to explain it all more precisely according to historical materialism.

Rather than using Marxist tools, and looking instead from a neoliberal perspective, it can be said that the workers are appropriating profits
that rightfully belong to the owner for having risked his capital and transformed it into machines and salaries, as opposed to stuffing it into a mat-
tress. In a sense, they are using machines that someone else purchased for
their own good, and this is no more justified than someone stealing a car
to use it as a taxi. The case of the recovered factories is different, however,
and the preceding arguments can be refuted – with their own logic.

In the first place, in nearly all the recovered factories, the owner owed
the workers back pay. This makes them into his principal creditors. In a
sense, they had "advanced" him unpaid work, at times enough to buy the
very machinery they used to produce.

Secondly, a good portion of the businesses were bankrupt or soon would be, which is to say that their owners were no longer their owners, or wouldn't be for much longer. In such cases, the justice system was in charge of ensuring that the creditors were paid as much as possible of what the owner owed them. In practice, what happens is that the creditors get little or nothing for the debts owed to them. Assets are sold at auction, and even in cases that don't involve fraud, they bring prices that are very low when compared to their real productive value.[94] These debts, as a co-op member said, are "virtual," and the real possibility of seeing them paid off is well-known to any creditor of a bankrupt business in our country. The properties, including any machinery left behind, are rated as empty buildings and not as potentially productive spaces. Generally, the only ones who can take advantage of the abandoned factory's potential value are the workers themselves. They're the ones that are most interested in seeing it continue to produce, but they lack the capital to buy the factory. To make things worse, it's not unusual for the person that buys the business at a fire-sale price to be a proxy for the original owner (who wants to recover "his capital" without taking responsibility for his economic mismanagement), or someone trying to keep the auction from working properly in order to pay almost nothing for the goods. While this isn't the way all businesses work, it was quite common in those that were later recovered.

Nor is it unusual for businesses that were later recovered to have received numerous subsidies and loans from the State, sometimes running into the millions of pesos. This was the case with Luiggi Zanón, among many others. This speaks to the reality that these capitalists aren't interested in being productive, but rather in making money, which is not necessarily the same thing. Many experiences have shown that investing in political contacts is much more advantageous than investing in technology or labor.

In short, there's a case to be made that the owners, in their race to maximize profits, extracted more than would have been possible with sustained productive practices, to the point of losing even their right to their own property. To put it another way, they advanced themselves the benefit that, in a best-case scenario, would have been obtained with more patience and attention to their work. In the words of Max Weber, these capitalists did not apply one of the facets of the spirit of capitalism, the asceticism that permits one to patiently accumulate the product of effort. It's as though, instead of selling a little milk from their cow each day, they sold all the milk the cow would produce throughout her life to different people, and promised the meat and leather to others as well. In practice, all those people can't reasonably expect to get what they were promised, because the cow

---

[94] As we saw before in the case of La Vasquita.

simply isn't worth that much. She will be worth more if she is milked reasonably, and is made to have calves, some of which go to meat and leather,
and others to produce more milk. In other words, she must work. In a
sense, this is what the workers of the recovered businesses are proposing:
making the businesses produce through old-fashioned work.

At first glance it might look like the workers are opposed to the fundamental presupposition of capitalism (private property), but in fact it is
the capitalist who is opposed to this presupposition. It is not necessary
to have a radicalized view of the matter to understand that what was
beneficial for the owners was not beneficial for society, or even fair, for
that matter.

Another important ingredient in the competitiveness of the recovered
businesses is the effect of the commitment of the worker to the business. The
capitalist dream is that the workers will "put on the uniform" to increase the
efficiency of the business, but that happens when the workers are part and
parcel of it. There are many examples of how the worker's commitment
can increase efficiency, as we saw above. In the Instituto Comunicaciones
Cooperative, a recovered school working within a club functioning under
bankruptcy laws, the president of the co-op explained to me:

> Now we can function with far fewer students, because much less money is wast-
> ed. There were many positions with high salaries for people who really didn't
> do anything, or at least whose presence is not missed. And there's more. For
> example, when the club showed me a gigantic water bill that the school owed, I
> took a close look at how the school could use 30m³ of water a month, even in the
> summer, when the school is closed. There, we saw that we were getting our water
> from a faulty connection drawing from two leaky tanks. The school is imposing
> a culture of efficiency on the club itself.

To give one example among many, we'll jump ahead to something
that Roberto Salcedo, president of the Union y Fuerza co-op, says several
pages from now:

> We're all the same. If a tool gets tossed aside, it's yours, too. You pick it up, you
> keep it. When there was a boss around, you kicked it aside or threw it where no one
> would see it. Before, if a machine broke, you called an engineer and sat down. Now,
> if it's about to break, you call the *compañeros* from maintenance and let them know
> it's making noise. If production stops, you don't get paid. You know it's yours.

This commitment is not just a negative thing; it has a positive
side as well. It is the workers who best know their jobs and can propose efficient innovations to improve productivity. Let's look at just
one example of how a recovered factory can grow. The former owners of the Zanón factory tried to fire a large portion of their workers,
had over US$75 million in debts (largely to the State), insisted that it

was external competition that was burying them, refused to pay salaries, and so on. Since being taken over by the workers, it's struggled
with gaining the trust of providers and buyers, a shortage of working
capital, and the fact that the business reopened during the worst of the
economic crisis. It has no lawyer to protect its work and lives under
the constant threat of eviction. In spite of all this, it's grown month by
month, and not only paid its workers, but hired 40 more, as its director,
a worker who didn't finish high school, notes. All this is possible thanks
to the explanation above. Even if getting rid of the owner cost alone is
not enough to make a business work and grow, it's a significant variable
in its chances for success.

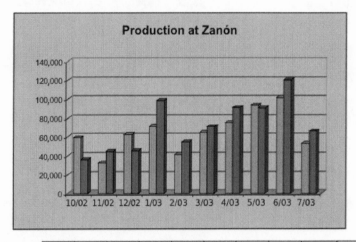

	10/02	11/02	12/02	1/03*	2/03	3/03	4/03	5/03	6/03	7/03**
Production	58,948	32,431	62,818	71,021	42,126	62,025	75,145	93,495	101,766	53,307
Sales	35,798	44,824	45,448	98,306	54,531	70,672	90,946	90,845	120,578	66,000

*Clarification: these statistics indicate production that had been fired, not all production. The
lowest average price per m² was AR$7.15. This amount varies according to product quality. A
m² of porcelain, for example, is AR$15. In cases where more of this product is sold, the average
tends to rise.*
   *   *The little bit registered in January was due to a contract with the Easy company for
         47,900 m² of material, which was scuttled by the former owners of the business.*
   *   *Only half the month is calculated.*

Clearly, workers can compete within the rules of the system, even
with many adversities arrayed against them. This is not a miracle – it
happens for clear-cut reasons, as laid out above. It should be pointed out
that in some cases, the workers are conscious that, despite achieving success within the system, it remains the same system that brought them to
the edge of the cliff and threw them into a battle whose outcome was

uncertain. These workers are not satisfied with the protective bubble they have managed to put around themselves. They have sampled the rare taste of doing what seemed impossible, and find it hard to keep working in their factories without trying to make an even deeper change.

3.3.2 The cost for the State

Another argument frequently used against the recovered factories when they ask for expropriations is that this would be an unjustifiable cost for the State, which is responsible for repaying the owner or the court holding the company in escrow, and that it has no assurance that it will recover any of that money. This and other legal attacks serve to undermine the methodology of putting factories under worker control.

Lawyers for the MNER give presentations in favor of the expropriations that include not only viability studies, but arguments demonstrating that the State benefits from assigning ownership to the workers, even if it has to pay indemnity to the former owner. Let's look at an example taken from a dairy factory that looked to the authorities to help the workers keep their jobs.

In this factory, there was a production plan showing the list of clients committed to buying products from the business once it was rehabilitated. This list was meant as an explanation of how the State would benefit from re-opening the factory:

> It should be pointed out that the present machinery of the cooperative allows it to employ 15 workers. Today, the investment needed to create a job in this industry is AR$100,000. That means that building the productive capacity of this factory would require AR$1,500,000. To dismantle this factory would cost the State AR$150,000 per year for unemployment insurance. And this factory brings in approximately AR$100,000 a month, which is a conservative estimate, considering that twelve months ago, it brought in almost AR$200,000 a month.

According to Dr. Kravetz, in three or four years the State earned back the cost of the indemnity, thanks to what it saved in unemployment subsidies and made by taxing production. And that's without considering the social impact of a functioning business.

The argument becomes weaker still if we consider the possibility that the businesses, expropriated according to viability studies, might emerge successful, enabling them to earn the money to pay back the State for the cost of indemnity. Anyway, it doesn't make much sense to spend too much time on this debate, as the recovered businesses will probably soon achieve some type of specific legal framework allowing them to stop using expropriation as a system to possess the means of production.

3.3.3 The lack of working capital

One of the topics dividing both movements is the need to finance the recovered businesses. When I asked Luis Caro about this, he said it was not necessary to ask anyone for loans, that the worker would, in time, be able to make everything work. In fact, this did happen in most of the factories (Zanón, Unión y Fuerza, Chilavert, Instituto Comunicaciones, etc.).

According to him, workers can, wherever necessary, begin to grow with no capital beyond their labor. He explains:

> In the factories, the engineers always talk to me about all the things needed to start working. I tell them they're wrong. All they need is work. The rest will come along, little by little. They get a few pesos together to connect the power and the gas, they get some raw materials however they can, and they start. Then it continues on its own.

In practice, what happens is that there are businesses that work at a small percentage of their productive capacity because they don't have the capital needed to take it to the next level. The bigger the factory, the greater the difficulty, because the balance point between costs and benefits is that much farther away. That's why businesses like FORJA San Martín waited for a loan to start production. In spite of it all, Zanón, with its capacity to produce a million m^2 of ceramics a month, started without capital and with 20,000 m^2 a month, and subsequently managed to grow. Clearly, this kind of beginning is hard for workers to imagine, and opinions vary widely on the topic. For example, Roberto Salcedo of Unión y Fuerza says:

> Our growth almost made a straight line from the beginning to today [August 2003]. Recently, we've been at 100%. We began with five or six tons a month, because we started up without capital. Clients came here who had nowhere to buy. We worked "*a façon*" – they brought us raw materials, we worked it and charged them labor. Over time, we invested that little bit of money in our own raw materials. Today, we have 180 tons. We had no subsidies or anything like that. What we have is a good policy: buy for two, sell for three. They've come here from the US Embassy, from the Ministry of Production, from lots of banks to offer us soft credit, but we didn't take any of it. We always had to offer guarantees, and to do that, we would have had to put our houses up. The thing is, the co-op didn't have a deed or anything. With this country as unstable as it is, with capital flight, the *corralito*,[95] the bad checks... If you get credit and then you can't pay it back, you end up losing everything. The guy from the embassy came by last week and told us they were starting to provide credit for all the cooperatives. And we told him

---

[95] Editor's note: The *corralito* is the name given to the policy enacted by President de la Rúa in December of 2001, whereby a strict limit was placed on the amount of cash that could be withdrawn from national bank accounts.

that unless we got really desperate, the truth was, we weren't interested. "What do you mean, not interested? We're not used to having people turn down our credit for growth." "We're growing, slowly but surely." "OK, but with credit, you could grow faster." "Yeah, we could grow faster, but we could also fall faster." Here, there's no race to grow. What was the objective? To keep our jobs, grow, tomorrow give our kids jobs, and take on new people. We don't want a race to make thousands of dollars tomorrow, and risk everything and end up with nothing. In this co-op, there's no need to think in black and white. We're betting on doubling production in two years. I think that's good growth, so it's not worth endangering what we've accomplished.

In many cases, this form of work can imply a degree of self-exploitation until a balance is reached by which there is enough volume to pay fixed costs and investment. In spite of it all, this situation is not generally met with dismay, since exploitation was previously not uncommon, and because the objective is to put an end to it once and for all. In fact, many cases, bad as they may be, still represent a material improvement over the conditions under the previous owners.

The workers in the most economically stable factories (such as Unión y Fuerza, IMPA, Zanón, Lavalán, etc.) have been able to pay themselves decent salaries, and even begun to expand to the point where they can bring new workers in to their cooperatives. In February, when I went to Chilavert, a printing press with eight workers, they told me they were drawing shares of AR$400. When I returned in May, they had fixed several machines, incorporated another worker, and were taking home AR$800 each. Ernesto, one of the workers there, also told me:

> The problem is that the old clients here were the Colón theater and foundations. The kind of work we do depends on re-establishing contact, the willingness of the authorities to keep us as a provider, and the budget. High-quality printing is expensive. So, now the market has changed. Now, it's common textbooks. Also, we don't have to go out [and drum up business] much, because we got so much press from the struggle that clients come to us.

There are other examples of factories, as we've seen, that have had trouble getting started. One of the Polo Obrero's specialists in recovered factories, Pablo Heller, summed up the conclusions of one of the meetings of the workers from the recovered factories:

> A common denominator among all the businesses is the lack of working capital. In the plenary session, and especially in the debates in the commissions, the different cooperatives restated their shortages. For example, the recovered mill in San Javier, in the north of Santa Fe, or the Baskonia metal foundry in La Matanza. In some cases, they've gotten credit from neighbors and organizations, but these are short-term and have to been repaid. Since they lack their own resources, the recovered businesses work '*a façon,*' which is to say, they are

commissioned by a third party, who generally advances them funds to buy the supplies, or directly provides the raw materials. This severely limits the growth of the cooperatives, and leaves open the possibility of their ending up prisoners of some business group.[96]

The solution proposed by the Polo Obrero is to get State help so these start-ups will not have to be returned.

The MNER seems to share the idea that the State needs to help, though in the form of loans. One of the explicit objectives for those struggling in this organization is the creation of a State fiduciary fund whose purpose would be to help kick-start production. In the meeting held in the middle of July 2003 in the BAUEN Hotel, a major topic of discussion concerned how to seek funds from different sources. In this particular case, there was talk about the possibility of setting up a €10 million fund with money provided by the Italian government, used to support businesses that needed investment.

---

[96] Heller, Pablo, "Análisis del Segundo Encuentro de Fábricas Recuperadas", available on the Partido Obrero website, 11/7/2002.

4. Conclusions

In a country where it's calculated that 30% of industrial capacity is idle and more than 30% of population is looking for work, the recovered factories have the resources and the space to grow. The fired workers, with their knowledge still intact, are capable of filling that space without recreating the conditions that brought on this last crisis. Within the many social movements that grew to the rhythm of the *cacerolas*,[97] the recovered factories have conditions that set them apart from the others. As admirable as the objectives of some of the *piquetero* movements may be, they began much further below, because they didn't have any machinery, productive experience or clients to recover. The same thing happened with the popular assemblies, at least those that survived and were able to find functions that transcended protest. The productive base of the recovered businesses makes them intrinsically different. In them, there's a way of life, and of producing life, which also implies novel rules on the inside. It could be said that these workers are stonemasons of a new reality in a place where the rules of exploitation don't exist.

Throughout 2003, some signs of improvement in the economy appeared, particularly a rise in exports. In spite of the expectations caused by this rise (of 16% in the first half of 2003, as compared to the same period in 2002), it should be pointed out that it isn't happening in sectors that have an impact on jobs, or on the redistribution of income. The overwhelming majority of this rise happened in industries, like soy, for example, that generate approximately 2.2 jobs for every million pesos produced; whereas textiles, for example, require 18 workers, shoes, 25. As if that weren't enough, soy or petroleum, the industries that have grown the most, take a good part of the profits directly out of the country. In the '90s, as was demonstrated, the increase didn't imply long-term growth, but rather a crisis in

---

[97] Editor's note: *Cacerolas*, or cooking pans, are a common tool of protesters, who bang them together to call attention to their cause.

the medium term. Improvements in the big numbers of the economy are not always all that much good.

At the other end of this spectrum, as we have seen, the recovered businesses find their reason for being in work. The benefits are distributed in an unusually equitable way among workers, and the money stays in the country. If the ruling classes don't take another look at the difference between policies of macroeconomic growth at any price (even semi-terminal crises) and those of growth for the benefit of society, the consequences could be completely devastating. Within the range of solutions capable of avoiding the repetition of the same errors, the recovered businesses should have an important place, as much for economic reasons as political and social.

Anyway, there's a big challenge waiting for those workers doing the "recovering." The first thing they face is the context in which they find themselves. Less than two years ago, Argentine society called into question the fundamental basis of the system. Everyone seemed ready to take the reins of the future into their own hands. Twenty months after the explosion, this has all become much blurrier. A right-wing major candidate –an elitist businessman – is able to collect almost 50% of the votes of a population that, two years earlier, took to the streets in massive numbers with the demand "Out with all of them!" The ladies who rapped the keys of their country homes against windows of the transnational banks, after a minimal social improvement, go back to looking mistrustfully at the *piqueteros*, scandalized because they block the path through the Plaza de Mayo, complaining about their misery. They can no longer manage to raise a hand in a protest song to show solidarity. The bourgeoisie, once again comfortable, stop looking upward critically. They once again begin to fear the lower rungs of the social ladder and the questions about "institutions" like private property.

Looking at this panorama, there's a sense that society flirted with rebellion for a time but, being elastic, returned to a Menemist normality – which ironically isn't normal, either. Reality, most likely, will settle somewhere between the two extremes. Within the context of this this tug-of-war, people have to be ready to compete in all fields, and the recovered factories represent the seed of something new that has the strength to triumph.

These factories are not going to disappear, nor will they go back to being what they were. The established ones could stop their journey toward questioning widely-accepted ideas, but it's safe to say they won't be able to go back to being more of the same. It's difficult to predict if factories will continue to open in significant numbers. Perhaps in a few years, we'll understand that those that exist were only possible thanks to a form of agonizing social organization. Perhaps the debacle, after taking a breath, will again attack virulently, and the workers will have to go out in massive numbers to work without asking for permission. The future in Argentina is extraordinarily unpredictable.

Then there are also threats that come from petty, small-minded politicians, eager to find genuine social movements from which to draw legitimacy. At least so far, as has been insisted on these pages, the recovered businesses mostly enjoy a healthy distrust, which keeps them immune to personal or outside interests. Still, accusations are exchanged between those that, in good faith or bad, start to see the political and economic potential to be had by he who controls this new form of production.

A co-op leader with strong political convictions was insistent with me during an interview about the differences between himself and other leaders of recovered factories. I made him see that the effort he was putting forth was excessive, because political dogmatism and co-optation (as we agreed) bring productive projects to an almost-inevitable failure. If the workers' independence at decision-making time really is an "adaptive advantage," there's no need to worry about attempts at co-optation. The workers are not naive (if they were, they wouldn't be working), and they know when they're fighting for a *compañero* and when they're doing it at the service of a political party that's only interested in power. This knowledge will choke some, but others will know how to learn from it. Internal disputes should be understood in the context of a country in which the only thing that outnumbers conspiracies is conspiracy theorists. That's why, throughout this book, there's been no special attention to the little fights of partisan political jockeying that acts as ballast, weighing down a new way of producing materially, socially, and politically – something that is genuine and unusual in our time, so marked by cynicism and downtrodden hopes.

Perhaps the toughest challenge for the future is to get more participants (judges, politicians, workers, the middle class, *piqueteros*, etc.) to open their minds enough to debate things from another angle, one in which the workers can succeed, in which a horizontal structure is possible, in which the lack of leaders is an advantage, in which solidarity is more effective than competition, and in which business prerogatives are questioned. It's impossible to convince, for example, Luiggi Zanón, of this. He only sees invading workers to whom he offered the possibility of work in a place that, decades ago, was a desert. The abuses he committed (from the workers' perspective) are, to him, the prerogatives of business owners as he imagines them. The real challenge is in establishing the idea in society that not paying salaries is not a capitalist's option, but rather a serious and potentially costly offense, and no less deplorable for being common. The challenge is to get judges to dialogue with the workers to understand what's happening in the factories. The challenge for society is to see citizens with rights, and not "pinko-ism" in its worst form (to use the famous phrase of Mirtha Legrand), behind each recovered factory and social advance.

For those that are anxious to bring about genuine social change, the recovered factories go back and forth between heaven and hell. One day, the pride of a worker describing his experiences carries us off to a heaven of optimism; the next day, a critical comment might drag us down into a hell of cynicism. To defend yourself against skepticism, it turns out to be necessary to get close to the factories that work, the ones where that poetic air is breathed, which journalists' articles so carefully try to reproduce. You need to see the overwhelmed expression of a worker who returns to HIS or HER factory after two years to find his own *mate* gourd in the same place where he left it. There's nothing wrong with giving yourself up once in a while to poetry and utopia, to occasionally, if only temporarily, renounce that "vulture look" which our society is so fond of, and which so often instills distrust and destroys good projects before they have the chance to blossom.

In any case, it's clear there's something new that should be welcomed and protected. With all the faults, defects and limitations recovered businesses may have, there are those who feel they've been born all over again. And that's enough to allow for joy and hope in each factory, school, hotel and clinic that opens in the hands of the workers.

And every day, you can find an excuse to celebrate. Just before the final corrections on this book were made, the workers scored another major victory in one of the most voracious of all fields: the mass media. The newspaper *Comercio y Justicia* in Córdoba was delivered into the hands of its workers under the perplexed gaze of the economic elites. The decision made by Judge Mansilla de Mosquera accepted the workers' offer to buy the newspaper at the base auction price and let them use the money owed to them as part of the payment (AR$400,000 out of a total AR$1,121,000). This is no small detail – it opens up the possibility that workers might in the future recover years of unpaid efforts in the best way: the possibility to continue working.

Only time will tell if what's being built is a path of alternative politics with an inalienably horizontal essence. For now, the author of this book is satisfied with the feeling of having provided some tools to think about new issues that might offer genuine alternatives to the paralysis of hope. Whatever may come, let's hope it will be in the hands of the workers, who continue laboring day by day, rebuilding a piece of society with their tools, almost without realizing it.

Esteban Magnani

August 2003
Almagro, Buenos Aires

5. THE SILENT CHANGE – AN UPDATE

About fours years after finishing the book you have just read, we can say the potential developments of the recovered factories phenomenon were properly foreseen. Recovered factories are still around, and the longer they have managed to produce the better they have become, in terms of machinery, salaries, client portfolio, and so on. There are also new recoveries taking place, a process that is speeding up at the time of writing these words, with the international crisis starting to gain momentum and now being felt in the Argentine economy. There have also been more attempts to bring the recovered factories together to turn them into a consistent movement, but with limited results. Also, along with the economic development, the political activities have receded to the inside of the factories, where the gymnastics of democracy seem to be more stable, both for better and worse. So what had been said four years ago about the prospectives of the phenomenon seems to have been accurate.

We have also finished the growth period that began five years ago and are on the verge of our once-every-ten-years crisis.[98] The challenge for the recovered factories, which grew in the context of a rising demand, will now be to prove they are able to compete in a market which has started to shrink. Also, the crisis is testing the words of Eduardo Murúa, who said that recovering factories have become a tool in the hand of the workers and that the tool would be used when the following crisis arrived. So far it is proving to be true: in the last two months there have been at least five occupations and at least two of the factories are already producing.

Anyway, this update does not intend to give a full picture of the situation of the recovered factories; probably the last comprehensive study

---

[98] For a better understanding of why the economic cycles in Argentina seem to be so short (about ten years instead of the usual 25 accepted as an average) I would suggest reading the following article (Spanish only): http://www.pagina12.com.ar/diario/economia/2-117974-2009-01-10.html.

of this kind was the one made by the UBA research group Facultad Abierta.[99] Rather, it will focus on providing an update of the trends foreseen in the previous book and the experience of the author, who has been working side by side with the cooperative workers for the last five years. This time it hasn't been as a mere observer, but as a supporting actor with a role in this development, thanks to a foundation called The Working World/La Base.[100]

5.1 The Working World/La Base

The history of La Base, as well as that of this book, is strongly related to the documentary "The Take," by Avi Lewis and Naomi Klein (see chapter 1.2). At the end of 2004, at a New York screening of the Canadian documentary, director Avi Lewis was approached by New Yorker Brendan Martin, who had studied economy and was an enthusiastic supporter of cooperativism, especially the Mondragón[101] model that had developed in large part thanks to a credit union fund. Brendan presented his own project of a financial network designed to promote democratic work and asked Avi if Argentina could be the place to make it come to life. When the documentary filmmaker showed his enthusiasm, they began to brainstorm for the birth of the non-profit organization.

This perception of the impact that a cooperative network could have on a region's economy was what motivated him to imagine a tool to strengthen cooperativism, and to keep this personal project for years while his working career led him into the world of computer programming. After some time, Brendan and Avi registered the Working World as a non-profit in the United States, to function as the organ receiving donations and managing the La Base Solidarity Fund. After settling in Buenos Aires, Brendan Martin contacted the people that had worked on "The Take" and started what was to become a fund for solidarity microcredit.

The first challenge was to prove the money had an impact, the businesses were viable and, last but not least, the workers wanted to pay back what was lent to them. After trial and error, the loan agents managed to help the cooperatives plan viable projects, ranging from buying raw materials to purchasing new machines for production. And from the beginning it was noticed that the workers wanted to pay back and have access to this new source of funding. That helped Brendan, the main fundraiser, show

---

[99] Facultad Abierta, 2005.
[100] For more information see wwwtheworkingworld.org.
[101] Editor's note: Mondragón is a large federation of cooperatives based in the Basque region of Spain. For more details visit http://www.mcc.es/.

enough good results to gain access to more money, ultimately increasing the fund and covering operating costs.

After two years working in the field designing and preparing productive projects with recovered factories and cooperatives of all types in the Buenos Aires area, the process of institutionalization began with a request for legal status of the NGO in Argentina, a status it finally obtained in June 2008 under the name La Base. This enabled other possibilities, such as an association with two other social organizations to apply for microcredit funds from the Argentine Microcredit Commission. Throughout this time, the Working World has strengthened its relationship with the country's cooperatives, and it plans to continue expanding its outreach to include the most geographically distant and those whose production levels require bigger investments. As of the end of 2008, we have completed more than a hundred loans and almost doubled the amount of loans and money provided every year.[102]

Thanks to this kind of work, all the members of the La Base team have experienced the challenges and success of everyday life in recovered factories.

5.2 The general context

As we said, the last four years in Argentina has been a period of consistent growth sustained in large part on a devaluation of the peso, a policy that increased the value of already high-priced commodities exported by Argentina, especially soybeans. The other leg of this model has been a constant support to keep the internal market high, boosting local industry, reducing unemployment significantly, and also reducing the social discontent, at least for the presidential term that began in 2003. These humble measures (it's debatable whether they could be called a "plan") allowed Argentina's GDP to grow 8.8%, 9%, 9.2.%, 8.5%, 8.5%, and 7% from 2003 to 2008 respectively (by the last quarter of 2008, there was a sudden stop in growth and some specialists already argue a recession is starting). Workers' income has grown consistently and sometimes even a little bit faster than inflation, the opposite of what had happened during the period of '90s neoliberalism.

As expected, wealth has not been distributed evenly. The difference between the rich and the poor has remained stable, meaning the rich have gotten richer and the middle class and some qualified workers have been able to increase their incomes. Of course they didn't all start from the same position, but their general situation has improved.

---

[102] For further details visit www.theworkingworld.org.

There are also many people that couldn't jump onto the train of growth, and it seems they won't be able to in the foreseeable future either (some would generally speak of 20% of the population, but the official figures for poverty are contested because the national statistics are constantly distorted by the national institution in charge, INDEC). They are the the fifth or sixth generation of unemployed families, with no "working culture," as we call it in Argentina. La Base worked with some cooperatives of this kind, which, despite having made a firm commitment to work hard and make the co-op profitable, couldn't achieve regular behavior patterns (such as waking up every day at the same time, not spending all the money as soon as they got paid, etc.) necessary for success.

On the other hand, the opposition of the middle class and the *Peronista* government of the Kirchners – whether created by the media, the Kirchners themselves, or a mixture of both – has changed the general reception for demonstrators and any political activity. The middle class, which in our opinion is the thermometer of our society even if they don't really represent the majority, seems to have accommodated to an improvement in living conditions and consumption levels and doesn't like the importance given to the working class by the government through transportation subsidies, increases in salaries, minimum pensions, price negotiations, etc., which, along with the neoliberal discourse, they consider the cause of inflation. Another middle-class symptom of this revulsion against Peronism and the affiliation to the neoliberal doctrine could be seen during the difficult and complex debates over an increase in the export taxes for agricultural products, basically the only source of money for the government to finance its policies. On the government side, it was argued that those revenues would allow the State to redistribute and invest in developing industry and would also keep the cost of food low and control inflation. The opposition maintained that an increase would ruin the producers (in fact, most of the production is being run by big transnationals that keep a good share of the profit and rent the land to locals), the "*campo*" (field producers). They also argued the *campo* represents Argentine roots and deserves respect, and that the government would simply steal the money or use it in a clientelistic way to maintain political power.

That kind of environment is certainly not the best for demonstrations, and it means a serious step back from the general support for social struggles, recovered factories included, that existed 8 years ago during the 2001 upheavals. The massive *piquetero* demonstrations have receded a lot since 2001, and they have been replaced by smaller demonstrations from a much more atomized set of demands, some of which address middle-class concerns such as "security." But generally speaking, demonstrations (especially if being held by the "others") tend not to be seen as reasonable by the media and the middle class unless the demonstrators are "the people" itself, meaning, of course, middle class people.

This change has had an impact on recovered factories, but the extent has been limited. The earlier support for activists at the beginning of the 21st century helped the workers build the political environment which would later allow them to get the expropriations. It was a costly political decision for deputies and senators in the moment, but the social context helped it to happen. That is not necessary any more, mainly for two main reasons. First, for most of the recovered factories, the struggle is in the market, not on the political grounds. The older recovered factories are trying to produce more and get more clients, and in the expanding market of the last five years, it wasn't as hard as it can be expected to be in the years to come. Second, the new takeovers already have the know-how and the legitimacy built by the previous recovered factories, which were able to show a much better success rate than what was initially expected by most of the politicians who lifted their hands in support of the expropriations. Back in 2001, expropriations were approved by desperate politicians, who needed to do something to control the fire and thought cooperatives wouldn't last for long anyway. As these pages are being written, there are at least five cases of new recoveries taking place, all using very different strategies. One of them is Indugraf, where the workers took over the factory, and which has since turned into a political "agora" where you can find *piqueteros*, left-leaning political parties, neighbors, politicians and all kinds of people visiting to enjoy the heat of the first days of a recovery. All those visitors also bring stories, contacts, support, and even food, helping to keep the struggle in high spirits and allowing the workers to appreciate the importance of what they are doing. On the other hand, there is a small factory, Esperanza del Plata, that has been recovered with a much lower profile (there is a second layer of recovered factories, especially in the suburbs of greater Buenos Aires, of which most people know nothing). It has just started to produce and to this point has had only the help of an activist and a lawyer with experience in recoveries and the know-how to deal with judges and politicians. In both cases, the previous experiences and confidence provided by successful examples allowed the workers to be hopeful about the future.

The success of the operating factories serves to increase the legitimacy of the recoveries and help these workers and others demand the use of these factories. Another reasonable point of view, held, for instance, by the lawyer Vanesa Castro Borda, who has assisted many recoveries, is that the State just wants to let this whole thing die away by not giving the movement any serious support. It could be just another expression of the State's lack of policies, but it has given time to the cooperatives to show what they are able to do, even if not in the best environment they could imagine.

The whole situation has therefore limited the social symbolic weight of the recovered factories as an alternative to capitalism but also has given some peace to the workers to focus on the economic challenges within a weak but relatively stable legal framework.

5.3 The movements

The limits for a serious institutionalization of the recovered factories, mentioned above, are still present. The Movimiento Nacional de Fábricas Recuperadas por sus Trabajadores (MNFRT) is still directed by the lawyer Luis Caro. The movement is still functioning and helps the workers with legal and accounting assistance and provides them a space to discuss common issues. However, except for a core group, there are many factories that, even feeling very thankful for the support received by the movement and its members, don't always accept its decisions or recommendations.

The way decisions are made and the political standpoint of Luis Caro have generated resistance not only among some cooperatives, but also from most of the activists and intellectuals related to the phenomenon. Some respected actors, such as Universidad Abierta, from UBA, have publicly declared a rejection of the MNFRT actions related to the control of the IMPA cooperative in 2004.

On the other hand, the Movimiento Nacional de Empresas Recuperadas (MNER) has disappeared. Eduardo Murúa's personalism, along with the lack of capacity of the movement to construct a solid project once the first conflict is solved, also generated resistance among the cooperatives. Murúa himself, respected in most of the cases for the support he showed to workers in the worst of conditions, has also been questioned for his stubborn attitude and lack of negotiation capacity. Recently he was even denounced by the BAUEN Hotel cooperative as trying to get involved in their conflict, taking the side of the former owners. Even if this sounds a little exaggerated, it gives an idea of the rejection he has generated in many cooperatives.

A new movement called FACTA (Federación Argentina de Cooperativas de Trabajo Autogestionadas), built mostly over the ashes of the MNER, has linked a more organized set of cooperatives from Rosario and the most "political" of the cooperatives in Buenos Aires. They have managed to set a lot of goals and achieve a fair number (such as getting a subsidy to create a fund for the cooperatives), but the internal tensions, mostly related to leadership conflicts, creates some skepticism about its future.

There is also the Consorcio del Sur, which gathers mostly metalworking factories in the southern area of Greater Buenos Aires. They have managed to set regular meetings where different political and economic projects are discussed. They have also secured the support of an Italian NGO that funds some of the projects. The political leadership in this case belongs to Francisco "Barba" Gutiérrez, the leader of one branch of the UOM (the Metalworkers Union)) and current mayor of the city of Quilmes.

5.4 The three pillars of the recovered factories

In this section we will try to provide an update for each of the main variables analyzed in the original book in 2003. We will go through the tendencies seen then and how many of them should be considered still significant.

5.4.1 The recovered society

One of the most interesting aspects of the recovered factories was the way it affected the workers, both the ones inside the cooperatives and the ones in other companies. I have had the chance to talk to some industrial workers that didn't have any direct connections to the recovered business-es but had heard about them and considered them a good thing. None of these workers, however, saw "recovery" as a real alternative toward which to strive. It still looks like the possibility of recovering a factory is some-thing that only becomes real when there are no other options – something that was seen in the first version of this book.

On the other hand, the recovered factories have had an unexpected impact on the value of cooperativism itself. Even if, as was said, starting a cooperative was just a way to get legal status to be able to put the factory back to work, it has turned into something valued that helps to frame the internal organization. This has also impacted other sectors of the society, which now value the idea of bringing their efforts together, cooperatively, as a tool to improve everybody's situation. Their struggles to create profit-able businesses deserve their own book, but let's just say that their starting point is lower than that of recovered factories. That has to do with many reasons, but primarily the lack of machinery (they don't inherit any, and have to buy it by themselves), the lack of working organizational experi-ence, and the lack of former clients, who already appreciate the quality of their product. Still, the appearance of a few middle-class cooperatives (such as SG and Cosem) or fast-growing examples (such as Desde el Pie or Puporé) with whom we at the Working World/La Base have worked, give hope for more added-value and skilled cooperatives.

The last and probably most important question, the one that raised the most expectations during the heat of the struggle: how did this new form of organization of labor impact the protagonist workers themselves?

As the reader might expect, there is no clear answer. From the experience of this researcher, there has been a huge variety of worker responses to their new situations. For most of them, even in the older recovered factories, their jobs are about making a living for their families, not changing society. Still, most of them value the way they work in the new cooperative environment; they feel proud of what they did, and most of them have learned to raise their voices when they don't agree with something. There is also a reasonable amount of accountability – when the information has been processed, which does not always happen – that has proved very important for the administration in terms of gaining legitimacy for their decisions and building support during assemblies. It could also be said that most of the workers still don't behave like cooperative members, but are somewhere between being employees and associates. I've especially found that many of the older workers still have the same tendency to make others give voice to what they want to say, or use gossip as opposed to more confrontational methods. This is totally understandable for people who have worked under a boss for decades and who have suffered the collateral damage of the many dictatorships that have attacked the working class with special ferocity.

There are special cases in which the political edge has to be kept sharp because the legal status is too weak, and that has created some political awareness among the workers. The constant visits from politicians, unions, and other workers organizations in BAUEN Hotel, for instance, keep the political side of the recovery constantly alert.

In recovered factories in general, the newer workers represent a source of doubts. When we talk about ex-workers joining the running cooperative, in most cases they seem to like it, especially the environment of camaraderie and small details such as free food, an understanding person in charge of managing human resources, work speed, etc. They get used to long night shifts when an unexpected order arrives. The cooperatives are focused not only on profit but also on working conditions, something that is very attractive for them. But when the cooperative doesn't need a particularly skilled person, they usually bring in a young relative. These young guys, in most cases, are working for the first time in their lives and are not used to the hard working rhythm of their new *compañeros*. So, even if the working conditions have improved they may find it hard to keep up with the pace of work. Especially in the metalworkers' factories the turnover is pretty high. On the other hand, the new workers usually only know about the struggle through references, as opposed to direct experience, and the pride and commitment is (perhaps understandably) lower.

In one particular metalworkers factory where they added 14 workers in one assembly (most of them had been on trial period for 1 or 2 years), after a few months the president was complaining that the new members had almost immediately grown more complacent and slowed down significantly their pace of work. He believed the improvement in their material situation had produced a direct negative impact on their productivity. He, who had been through his cooperative's hard, long and violent struggle, felt disappointed by this perceived drop-off and expressed fear that the solid project they had built would fall apart as the older workers started to leave the factory. Though not a truly representative sample, this can help to imagine the new challenges the more successful recovered factories will have. In any case, it is completely understandable that the new members don't come from a vacuum, but from a society in which success is something largely achieved by individuals, not groups. Once again, we have to remember that cooperativism in Argentina, unlike in Spain or Italy, has grown out of necessity, and as such the education issues have not been given too much attention.

5.4.2 Recovered legislation

What's new in the legal scene of the recovered factories? Not much. At most, as lawyer Florencia Kravetz[103] argues, some judges in charge of bankruptcies changed their view about the viability of the cooperatives and the workers right to use the factories. Therefore, they have started to consider the cooperatives as a viable alternative to the auction block and are more willing to give the workers rights to productive continuity. Some of them even use other legal arguments to extend the permission to use the factories arguing rights and laws that contradict the bankruptcy law. In other cases, the judges argue that the law has always been the same and it is clear that they have a certain amount of time to sell the assets through an auction and pay the creditors. For them, court is not the right place to challenge a law and change the system. In Argentina, the judges in charge of the bankruptcies are chosen at random, so in that lottery the workers can either win or lose a lot of time and effort.

In fact, the creditors in any normal bankruptcy rarely get much of their money back, and there have been very few cases in which they have been active in trying to recover lost money. As Florencia points out, the appointed trustees, the ones in charge of selling the remaining assets and the ones who get paid first when the mission is accomplished, are, in most cases, the same ones interested in pushing the case forward. She argues that she has tried to explain to many appointed trustees and creditors that they had a better chance of getting their money back if they pushed the State to pass the expropriation law and get it to pay for the compensation. So far, she's had no luck with this.

---

[103] She is the same lawyer interviewed in the original text. She has continued working with the recovered factories, although she has been questioned in some of them and left.

As mentioned above, only a couple of exceptional cooperatives managed to have the compensations paid to make the expropriations definitive and legally stable. They still have to pay back that money to the government as if it were a mortgage, but the terms and interest rates are soft and they should be able to deliver on time. But for the majority of the recovered factories, as mentioned above, the only option has been to extend the expropriation to give more time to the State to pay the compensation. That just kicks the ball forward and gives more time to the co-ops to consolidate their projects, though it does still leave them in a legal limbo. If the political decision to actually pay for the compensations doesn't arrive, more struggles will take place. The BAUEN Hotel case shows an extreme example of this situation: BAUEN never managed to get the expropriation and there has been a solid eviction order for months, but no authority wants to pay the political cost of putting more than a hundred workers on the streets. To make it even more complicated, BAUEN workers have always been aware of their delicate position and have been building political networks with all kinds of political actors: unions, political parties, politicians, social movements of unemployed, etc. If there were an eviction, besides the complication of sending the police into a 15 floors building full of tourists, there would be huge demonstrations 10 blocks from the *Obelisco*, the very symbolic center of Argentina. That is an extreme case, but if no definitive solutions are taken, there could be many BAUENs all around the city.

So where can a solid solution be found? There are few measures that could help. First of all, the State should pay for the compensations and give the workers the possibility to pay it back. The more solid co-ops, the ones that take the projects seriously and "deserve" their factories, will deliver and become the definitive owners of the assets. The second measure would be a credit line for recovered factories to give the cooperatives a chance to survive. This access to capital is a very basic need without which there is very little long-term chance for success. And the third measure, thinking mostly about the future, is to make a serious change in the bankruptcy law to allow the workers to make use of their constitutional right to work. The other main change the law needs is to permit the workers to exchange the labor debts owed them (unpaid salaries, taxes, pensions, etc.) for factory assets. As mentioned above, there has been one case in which that happened, but it turned out to be a huge exception that has never been repeated. Another alternative for that law could be to allow the workers to pay a rent for the assets. That rent could then be used to pay creditors.

On the other hand, as Florencia acknowledges, the workers should also understand that sometimes it's easier to move into a small factory, even if they have to pay rent, than to try to justify that they are in charge of a huge space which might take years to become profitable and pay for itself. In those cases, it would be smarter to just take some of the machinery to a space more suitable for their real needs and possibilities. Putting that option in the balance of the negotiation could allow the workers to end up with a good deal.

When asked about the future of the recovered factories if nothing were to change, if there were no political decision to pull the recovered factories out of legal limbo, Florencia answered that she would expect about 70% to resist and survive in the long term. That ratio could certainly go up if the political environment helped them with a few measures.

5.4.3 The recovered economy

When the first version of this book was written the political and legal struggle was at its peak. Only a few recovered factories had more than three years working experience to return economic balance to their factories. The oldest ones, such as Unión y Fuerza, were trying to stabilize themselves. Since then, the only representative study on relevant economic variables was the one done by Facultad Abierta.[104] It concluded that the older the cooperative, the better the income, something that seems to this writer to be a very good rationale for measuring success. Even without a statistical approach, but with a deeper knowledge of the cooperatives' finances as compared to 4 years ago, my own experience verifies the hypothesis.

When I interviewed Roberto Salcedo, president of Unión y Fuerza, in 2003, he said that with a shopkeeper's accounting ("I buy for two, I sell for three") they had managed to grow and were planning to buy the building next door to double the amount of workers and production. It looked far too optimistic. But when I met him again in 2008, he told me that they had achieved those goals and had to clean a space next to the factory to park the cars of the now 110 members, most of whom had bought new autos in the last few years. They had wisely chosen to get help by paying a consultant and wound up with the technical assistance of INTI (National Institute of Industrial Technology). They were even concerned about the transnational exploitation of national copper, their main cost, and the consequences it had on the local market; they were planning to do something about it. Only workers who have already put a factory back to work would try to deal with the international mafia of the companies managing the metal business in Argentina.

We have to say that probably Unión y Fuerza is not the most representative case, but on a smaller scale cooperatives like Crometal, Metal Varela, RB, Rabbione, Campichuelo, Cintoplom, La Nueva Esperanza (ex-Global), Huesitos de Wilde, etc., most of whom are relatively young,

---

[104] Facultad Abierta, 2005.

have managed a growth from zero production to providing a decent wage or more for all of their members. Depending on their branch of production, board capacities, access to capital and a few other variables, most of the recovered factories have managed to grow at least in the recent context of general economic growth. Furthermore, I haven't heard of any recovered factory that was dissolved after restarting production.

How is this possible? Once again, the variables mentioned in the first version of the book (see chapter 3.3) are still the answer. These companies, most of them bankrupted or closed for not being profitable anymore, were abandoned by the owners, but the workers stayed and managed to make a living out of them. It should be clear to everyone that the departure of the businessmen has to have something to do with that subsequent success. The main and most obvious explanation is that the personal profit for the owner is being redistributed among the workers or reinvested in the factory: the profit margin, meaning a certain amount of money that has to be taken from the company to maintain the lifestyle of the owner, doesn't exist anymore as such.

The other side of the coin is that the source of capital is also gone. As we pointed out before, the lack of access to capital is a serious limitation to the cooperatives as businesses. Banks don't lend money to workers unless they have some collateral. As the cooperatives don't own the factories (they just have permission to use the assets) they have nothing to show the banks. To confront this challenge, a few cooperatives accepted taking on an investor, who in some cases has turned into a new private management, allowing the co-op to survive but concentrating power in his own hands. In other cases, the cooperatives have received subsidies, orders from the State, money from some good friend or credit from the Working World/La Base or another NGO. This has allowed them to slowly start to build up enough working capital to grow. But probably the most common source of capital has been some type of self-exploitation.

On the other hand and for the first time, in the last couple of years the State has finally payed for expropriations (such as in the case of Cooperativa Vieytes, ex-Ghelco, part of Maderera Córdoba, Mecber) with loans the cooperatives have to pay back in twenty or so years with two or three years of grace. That has been a huge step forward, because it seems once a few examples exist, subsequent cases need a lot less work to achieve the same goals.

The other source of success for the recovered factories mentioned above was the commitment of the workers to save resources and time. Even the members of the coops who are not totally committed to cooperativism have internalized that if a machine breaks, it's reasonable to try to get it back to work as soon as possible. Even if the commitment with the cooperative doesn't come from inside them, workers start to understand that their own salaries depend on their production. When La Base

submitted to the General Assembly of Cooperative Metal Varela an accounting analysis of how much they had to produce to be able to pay costs
and increase salaries, the attitude of workers towards productivity issues,
previously rejected, changed to a better understanding. The cooperative
then spent two months focusing on these goals, and to the delight of even
the most reluctant to the idea of cooperativism, profit margin increased
significantly. The trend didn't always continue, but mainly because of demand problems. Anyway, these kinds of activities clearly have an impact,
but they are not that common, mainly because that kind of information is
just not available (in the case of Metal Varela, it had been done by a member of Metal Varela with the assistance of a former member of La Base,
accountant Eleonora Feser) or because the administrative board has problems with sharing information. Still, with all these limitations, the attitudes
of the workers towards their jobs tend to be consistently different from the
way it was in regard to production. That is even clearer when the line that
unites their production with their salaries is made explicit.

As mentioned above, the psychosis of State policies have allowed some
of the cooperatives to start paying for the assets they are using thanks to
loans from the national banks. This is both a step forward and a challenge,
because even in the best conditions, the payments of those loans will certainly have an impact on the recovered businesses.

5.5 Conclusion

I once read that an intellectual, when asked on TV about the consequences of the French Revolution, answered "It is too early to say."
The recovered factories have the same problem and will for a long time.
Cooperative movements with about 50 years of experience, like the
Mondragón model in Spain and Emilia Romagna in Italy, still face challenges, and some may consider they have failed (in cooperative terms) in
spite of their (economic) success. So, even if it will always be too early to
make a final analysis, there are a few things that can give us an idea of the
current situation of recovered factories.

First off, they have shown that they are economically viable and socially
desirable. Compared to the reception they had a few years ago in the con-
servative scene, most economists and journalists had to accept that they had
managed to survive. They may still argue they did it out of self-exploitation
or simple theft, but they have to accept they've found a way through.

Also, there has been a considerable impact on other workers. As has
been mentioned many times throughout this book, recovering the workplace has turned into a viable option, and in hard times, like those starting
now, it has been chosen by many workers.

On the other hand, a deep change in Argentine society, for example the way money and power is distributed, is something that recovered factories will certainly not do by themselves. However, they could fit perfectly into a more egalitarian society. And, it has to be said that the political class in Argentina, since the chants of "que se vayan todos" during the 2001 upheavals, has been able to recycle itself just enough not to change the main trends of distribution. The transnational companies and the large national companies, plus some other sectors such as mining and privatized services companies, with their strong connections to the political class, are still the ones pulling the strings of Argentina's fate, regardless of how much they complain about the Left taking over the country.

But in the micro-politics of the recovered factories, where the workers try everything to make their own cooperatives work, developing creativity to make their cooperative profitable is a huge step forward for democracy. As said before, having the workers finally taking their future in their own hands and doing something with it, without any preceding foreign intellectual framework, can have some unexpected results, and they are enjoying the trip. So are we.

February 2009
Almagro, Buenos Aires

Bibliography

"Abrecaminos", N°1 magazine, december 2002.

"Ocupar, Resistir, Producir" magazine, MNER", N° 1, November 2002.

Allegrone, Verónica; Partenio, Florencia y Fernández Alvarez, María Inés, "Ocupaciones fabriles: un rastreo de las experiencias históricas", presentation for the "VI Congreso Nacional de Estudios del Trabajo", August 2003.

Battistini, Osvaldo (comp), "El trabajo frente al espejo", Prometeo libros, Buenos Aires, Argentina, 2004.

Caro, Luis, "Las empresas en crisis. La expropiación de plantas fabriles en una salida viable" publication from the MNFRT, 2003.

Carpintero, Enrique y Hernández, Mario (compilers), "Produciendo Realidad", Topía Editorial, 2002.

Carracedo, Orlando, "Economía Social Agraria", Depalma, Buenos Aires, 1984.

Cavallone Brebbia, Adolfo, "Cooperativismo. Sociedades Cooperativas en la República Argentina", Semca, Buenos Aires, 1947.

Chaves, María; De Rissio, Julieta; Di Fino, Mariano; Lesser, Pablo; Rauch, Magdalena; Sparacino, Ariel; "Brukman: bajo control obrer@", 2002.

Equipo de Educación Popular, "Obreros sin Patrón", Ediciones Madres de Plaza de Mayo, Buenos Aires, Argentina, 2005.

Facultad Abierta, "Las empresas recuperadas en la Argentina", Seube-UBA, Buenos Aires Argentina., 2005

Fajn, Gabriel (coord.), "Fábricas y empresas recuperadas", Centro Cultural de la Cooperación, Buenos Aires, Argentina, 2003.

Fernández Alvarez, María Inés "Transformaciones en el mundo del trabajo y procesos de ocupación/ recuperación de Fábricas", presentation for the "I Jornadas de Interfases entre Cultura y Política en Argentina IDES", 17 - 18/12/2002.

Gil de San Vicente, Iñaqui, "Cooperativismo obrero, Consejismo y Autogestión Socialista", published in Internet (http://www. basquered.net/cas/revol/gilo2/coop.htm), 2002.

Heller, Pablo, "Empresas ocupadas, gestión obrera y cooperativas", available at: http://www.poloobrero.org.ar/sindical/gestionobrera/descomposicion.htm, 20/06/2002.

Heller, Pablo, "Fábricas ocupadas y gestión obrera", taken from the magazine "En defensa del Marxismo" magazine, year 11, N°30, Ed. Rumbos, April 2003.

Heller, Pablo, "Análisis de las leyes de expropiación de Ghelco y Chilavert. La clase no obrera no necesita el paraíso", Polo Obrero site in Internet, September, 2002.

Henry, Michel, 1984, «La vie, la mort. Marx et le marxisme», «Diogène», No125, magazine.

Indymedia article, "Nueva provocación en Zanón", (http:// argentina. indymedia.org), 7/10/2002.

Johnston Birchall, Co-op, "The People's Business", Manchester University Press, Manchester, UK, 1994.

Lannot, Jorge; Amantea, Adriana y Sguiglia, Eduardo; "Agustín Tosco. Presente en las luchas de la clase obrera", TGS, March 1999.

López Echagüe, Hernán, "La política está en otra parte", Editorial Norma, Buenos Aires, Argentina, 2002.

Mandel, Ernst "Control obrero, consejos obreros, autogestión", Ediciones La Ciudad Futura, Buenos Aires, 1973.

Marx, Karl, 1968, "The German Ideology", Progress Publishers, 1968.

Mateo, Graciela "El cooperativismo agrario en la provincia de Buenos Aires (1946-1955)", from "Mundo Agrario" magazine, N° 4, La Plata, 2002.

Meyer, Adriana, "Quiénes son los jueces que ordenaron el desalojo", Página/12 newspaper, 24/3/03.

Mohamad, Jorge, "Recuperación y autogestión de fábricas en crisis", RYC Editora, 2006.

Palomino, H (compiler),"El movimiento de trabajadores de empresas recuperadas", from Relaciones de Trabajo studies, Facultad de Ciencias Sociales (UBA), January, 2003.

Pérez Crespo, Guillermo, "Las herramientas legales en la lucha sindical", in "De eso no se habla", TEL notebooks, January 2003.

Petras, James and Veltmeyer, Henry "Autogestión de trabajadores en una perspectiva histórica", in "Produciendo Realidad. Las empresas comunitarias", Carpintero, Enrique y Hernández, Mario, Ed. Topía, 2002.

Petras, James,"Argentina: 18 Months of Popular Struggle – A Balance", available at http://www.rebelion.org/petras/english/030604petras.pdf, 28/5/2003.

Rebón, Julián y Saavedra, Ignacio, "Empresas Recuperadas", 2006, Capital Intelectual, Buenos Aires, Argentina.

Rebón, Julián, "Desobedeciendo el desempleo", Ediciones Picaso, Buenos Aires, Argentina,2004.

Rebón, Julián, "La empresa de la autonomía", Ediciones Picaso, Buenos Aires Argentina, 2007.

Rizza, Roberto, Sermasi, Jacopo, "Il lavoro recuperato", 2006, Bruno Mondadori, Milano, Italy.

Sienrra, Celestino (h). "Campo y ciudad. El problema agrario argentino", Buenos Aires, La Vanguardia, 1946.

Tugendhat, Ernst "Ser - Verdad - Acción", Editorial Gedisa, Spain, 1998.

Vales, Laura, "Los desmanejos financieros amparados por la justicia", Página/12 newspaper, 19/5/03.

Vales, Laura, Hacher Sebastián, in "Nuestra Lucha" magazine, N°91, June 2003.

Wright, Mills, "De hombres sociales y movimientos políticos", Ed. Siglo XXI, 1969.

3417029

Made in the USA